GREAT NEW ZEALAND RAILWAY JOURNEYS

GREAT NEW ZEALAND RAILWAY JOURNEYS

GRAHAM HUTCHINS

EXISLE
PUBLISHING

First published 2008

Exisle Publishing Limited,
P.O. Box 60-490, Titirangi, Auckland 0642, New Zealand.
'Moonrising', Narone Creek Road, Wollombi, NSW 2325, Australia.
www.exislepublishing.com

National Library of New Zealand Cataloguing-in-Publication Data

Hutchins, Graham.
Great New Zealand railway journeys / Graham Hutchins.
ISBN 978-1-877437-28-1
1. Railroad travel—New Zealand. 2. Scenic railways—
New Zealand. 3. New Zealand—Description and travel.
I. Title.
919.304—dc 22

Cover and text design by Nick Turzynski, redinc., Auckland
Printed in China through Colorcraft Ltd., Hong Kong

Photo acknowledgements

The publishers thank the copyright holders of photographs in this book:
Tony Bridge: pp. 2-3, 6, 25, 29, 30, 32, 33, 35, 39, 40, 43, 45, 46, 61, 65, 66, 70, 72, 75, 87,
88, 90, 95, 96, 98, 99, 103
Mike Harding: p. 170
Graham Hutchins/Russell Young: pp. 26, 37, 49, 53, 56, 62, 97, 101, 104, 125, 129, 131, 151, 161
Niall Robertson: pp. 51, 68, 81, 92, 105, 108, 112, 114, 115, 118, 121, 124, 167, 171, 173
D. R. Simpson: front cover, pp. 16, 23, 143, 155, 158, 159, back cover
K. B. Ward: 36, 133, 136
The Kingston Flyer: 11, 14, 21
Napier City Council: 127
Tranz Scenic: pp. 67, 71, 85, 123, 140, 144, 165
Wellington City Council: 117
Exisle Publishing: 141

PREVIOUS PAGE: The TranzCoastal scythes through the dry north Canterbury countryside.

CONTENTS

INTRODUCTION

For some passengers train travel is simply a means of getting from A to B; from home to work or school and back again. Others travel on trains because of the ease of passage, the conviviality of fellow passengers, or the stimulation of meeting tourists from an expanding range of cultures.

Then there are those who regard train travel as an almost spiritual or other-worldly experience, whose vision goes beyond even the practical belief that this is the way human beings should travel: confined to singing steel lines while rogue cars and buses grapple with opposing traffic. Or contending with the often brutal transit of airlines, beset in this century with protracted security measures and sardine-tin confinement.

For such enthusiasts, train travel is not just the only way to go. In itself it is one of the western world's most profound pleasures.

Globally, train travel is on the increase. Even in New Zealand there is evidence of resurgence. The era of retrenchment brought about by the motor car and the aeroplane and later, the spurious blip of market-driven rail sales and closures, is giving way to more pro-rail considerations. In mid 2008, the Labour government bought back the rail system to complete the foundations of resurgence.

Tourism has become a critical revenue-earner for New Zealand. Matchless and varied scenery, an equitable climate, friendly people and a certain laid-back ambience have been cited by visitors as reasons for the increasing popularity of this country as a holiday destination. And tourists expect to be able to see a goodly proportion of the country from a train window. It's what they are used to at home.

The axing of the Southerner passenger service from Christchurch to Invercargill was a retrograde step in 2002. Spirited opposition to the closure wasn't enough to halt the tide of market forces. There was a mood of helplessness abroad that did the country no favours. In the five years since the loss of the Southerner there has been a hardening of resolve. The importance of tourism has become embedded in the national psyche, along with a dawning awareness of the importance of trains in the equation.

It was as much the vested interests of tourist operators and beneficiaries served by the Overlander as a general sense of foreboding among a broad cross-section of Kiwis, that caused the widespread revulsion at the decision in 2006 to cancel the Overlander. The realisation that ideologues committed solely to commercial considerations were about to kill off another Kiwi icon – the daily train service along the mythical North Island Main Trunk line – led to a stirring in the hearts and minds of thousands. The cancellation of the service would have led to haemorrhaging credibility in the halls of power.

OPPOSITE The TranzCoastal at Kaikoura. Passengers alight to watch whales and other marine life.

Interested parties came to the rescue financially and the Overlander was saved.

A younger generation of rail administrators and policy-makers, who may have taken up their new rail management portfolios thinking a train was something you saw at weddings, had to be brought up to speed. Not that the Overlander was a fast train, but it represented timeless aspects of New Zealand's European past and pointed unequivocally to the future.

The journeys covered in this collection are as much about history as the here and now. The Kingston Flyer, Taieri Gorge Railway Limited, Johnsonville suburban train and Weka Pass Railway vintage operation run on slivers of abandoned state lines. In doing so they inevitably conjure up the colourful past of an official network that played a unifying role in opening up isolated regions of a young country. In 1953 the New Zealand rail system, all 5,656 km of it, reached its apex.

Great railway journeys do not have to traverse continents or bisect nations to be memorable, although they sometimes do and are. Nor do they have to occupy three days and two nights while threading canyons, straddling mountain ranges and crossing several time zones. Some New Zealand train journeys have been nominated as among the most dramatic in the world thanks to the country's compressed physical grandeur and diversity. This is never more apparent than when travelling on the TranzAlpine between Christchurch on the east coast of the South Island and Greymouth on the west. It is even possible to do the return trip in a single day, through scenery that encompasses plains, foothills, mountain ranges, river gorges and glistening wetlands. If you blink you miss something momentous.

Similarly, the resurrected Overlander negotiates such diverse landscapes through the heart of the North Island in less than 12 hours that many tourists repeat the journey from Auckland, New Zealand's largest city, to Wellington, the capital. Or vice versa. Sensory scenic overload means another ticket is required to take it all in.

Each journey in this collection is unique. The Overlander, the award-winning TranzAlpine, and the TranzCoastal, which has garnered a reputation as one of the world's most arresting sea-girt jaunts, are regarded as the flagbearers of New Zealand train travel. They certainly cover the longest stretch of track, yet length of passage is not the only measure of their appeal.

The Kingston Flyer and Weka Pass Railway are windows on the past. If you hanker after seeing New Zealand in the steam era, such round trips are akin to travelling on moving museum pieces. If you are simply along for the ride, the scenic contrast between mountain-shrouded plateaux and limestone-studded Canterbury hill country is typical of New Zealand's compacted scenic grandeur.

Also in the South Island, the Taieri Gorge Railway highlights river gorges with distinctive schist landscapes and elevated encroachments along the picturesque Otago coast.

Further north, the train from downtown Wellington to Masterton in the Wairarapa relives the age of the provincial express and railcar, although now its versatility shows in its mix of commuters, everyday travellers and growing groups of tourists. Such services were as 1960s as All Black Colin

Meads. From the city and suburban reaches, through the 8.7 km Rimutaka Tunnel and past sparkling Lake Wairarapa, the train ambles through a rural hinterland studded with refurbished rural towns before pulling into the archetypal provincial town of Masterton.

Wellington's suburban Johnsonville branch, running through the heart and spine of a physically unique city, is like no other. Traversing the initial stages of the original North Island Main Trunk, the bush-clad, circuitous climb not only summons up the past but gives a nod to the future. It is both scenic and pragmatic. It winds above gorges and through attractive wooded enclosures, yet does the job of getting commuters to where they have to be.

Another Wellington-based commuter train, the Capital Connection to Palmerston North is the future: a designated city-to-city, long-distance commuter service with many of the sophisticated trappings destined to be applied to similar commuter trains in other New Zealand cities. Particularly Auckland, where the upgrading of the western line, domain of the delightfully eccentric train to Waitakere, proceeds apace. Here artists and freethinkers lurk, secure in the knowledge that their train will soon be enhanced by electrification, double tracking and new stations.

Beyond regular, scheduled services, excursion trains have taken up the slack and held the line. In the years since passenger trains were withdrawn from significant tourist traps like Northland, Bay of Plenty, Hawke's Bay, Taranaki and that vast stretch of the South Island once served by the Southerner, organisations like Steam Incorporated, Mainline Steam Trust, Feilding and District Steam Rail

Society, the Railway Enthusiasts' Society and the Taieri Gorge Railway have operated popular excursion trains to destinations no longer served by regular services.

One of the more colourful excursion jaunts is the annual 'Art Deco' train that travels from Paekakariki to Napier, initially up the main trunk, then through the Manawatu Gorge and out into the scenic Hawke's Bay hinterland. The Hawke's Bay line last saw regular passenger services in October 2001 when the Bay Express terminated, but the excitement generated by the Art Deco Express every February as it carries celebrants to Napier's Art Deco Weekend, gives every impression of being a daily event. And it is steam-hauled.

The past mingles with the present. The current fascination with steam-drawn services has proved to be more than the mere dalliance of an older generation. Young tourists are just as chuffed with the puffing monsters at the business end of the train. The Kingston Flyer is exclusively steam-hauled, the Weka Pass Railway only relegates its immaculate A428 steamer in times of fire risk in the hinterland. Even the endangered Overlander now tacks steam engines on the front of some of its services. The functional, fun-less diesels are dropping back in the motive force pecking order.

Whether steam-hauled, diesel-driven or electrically-propelled, these railway journeys are not simply a celebration of trains that have survived in the New Zealand scheme of things. They each have their own distinctive character and stamping ground, and in many ways foreshadow a more general appreciation of what lies ahead for New Zealand train travel.

① VOLCANO ON WHEELS: THE KINGSTON FLYER

KINGSTON TO FAIRLIGHT

The Kingston Flyer is a steam-drawn tourist train that is an icon of the New Zealand transport landscape. Certainly its season is confined to the months between 1 October and 30 April in any given year and these days it stretches out over little more than 14 km of preserved track, between the village of Kingston and the locality of Fairlight in Southland, yet it retains a certain mystique, based on a wonderful history, and remains easy on the eye.

PREVIOUS PAGE Working up a head of steam, the Kingston Flyer is about to depart Kingston, bound for Fairlight.

There is a great deal of the romance of the railways associated with the Kingston Flyer. At the outset the Lady Barkly, a steam engine named after the wife of the Governor of Victoria, was the first locomotive to take tentative steps in this country, at the tail end of the line that has historic connections with the Kingston-Invercargill rail route and the Kingston Flyer. And for many years the Kingston Flyer carried holidaymakers to the Central Otago resort centres, most notably Queenstown, utilising the lake steamer connection from Kingston. An element of excitement was attached early to the meanderings of the Flyer, in days when rail was the most efficacious manner of getting through. Even in the early days of the link, weekend excursions were a speciality: a chance for women to don their finery and men to tweak their moustaches at the romantic prospects.

The discovery of gold around Lake Wakatipu in 1862 was the magnet that advanced the route north from New Zealand's deep south. There was romance inherent in that, and the rails from Bluff, where the Lady Barkly chuffed nervously, headed due north.

It was not love at first sight. The original line from Bluff at the very bottom of the South Island was made of wood. Roads north out of the province had proved heavy going because of the swampy terrain and a railway, albeit wooden, was seen as a panacea. Inevitably the wooden rails succumbed to the marshlands and heavy rain. On the very first day of operation an excursion train became cast on the slippery white pine rails. Their Scottish heritage and a certain meanness with money had convinced Southlanders that the cheaper wooden option made economic if not practical sense.

The authorities had been silly enough to oversee the extension of the wooden line as far north as Makarewa, 12 kms beyond Invercargill. But as the line continued to present problems, thoughts soon turned to conventional steel track. After three years of unromantic nonsense, the wooden rails were replaced in 1867 with steel. The lure of Wakatipu gold, long unable to get a grip, returned.

The construction of the line was celebrated every time the railhead was extended and another milestone reached. Reports of cavorting and 'improvised sports' after over-indulging were common as this 'romantic' line extended northwards. Gentlemen were held to account by concerned wives as the line inched towards the mecca of Kingston and Lake Wakatipu, where gold — or what was left of it — and good times abounded. The Terminus Hotel at Kingston became a railhead beacon.

It was a red-letter day when the final link to Kingston was officially opened in 1878. A steamer ferried in guests from Queenstown. A train consisting of 20 packed carriages behind four locomotives arrived from Invercargill. The rocky outcrops marking the southern end of the lake reverberated with the clamour of it all. Tales of revelry and high humour echoed around the colony. On the homeward journey several carriage axles were smoking hot in the excitement of the occasion. Not that the revellers neglected their duty to their fellow man. Not far from Winton an injured sawmill worker was laid out gingerly in a carriage aisle and accompanied the merry throng back towards Invercargill Hospital.

Ironically, the first Kingston Flyer plied a new line from Gore to Lumsden across the Waimea Plains, and then on to Kingston. This initiative had come about when the citizens of Dunedin, intent on taking advantage of Wakatipu gold, added to the rivalry between Otago and Southland by opening the Waimea Plains line in 1880.

The first Flyer was a fast train by New Zealand standards. It represented a 'rail rush' almost as heated as the initial scramble for gold. In later years as the gold deposits dwindled it slowed down.

Meanwhile the connection between Invercargill and Kingston had been completed and thanks to a mixed train service Invercargill folk could share the excitement of travelling north to the holiday playgrounds around Lake Wakatipu. The Invercargill to Kingston link was regarded as part of the main South Island trunk system extending from Christchurch, via Invercargill and north again to Kingston, so although Southlanders did not share in the romance associated with the original Kingston Flyer that emanated from Gore, they could glory in their main trunk categorisation, at least in the early years. The Invercargill-Kingston line retained its revised status as a secondary main line up until the 1950s.

The concept of the Kingston Flyer when it was reinvented in 1971 was a little bottler. Steam engines had just petered out on New Zealand Rail services and some far-sighted soul figured there would be a residual sadness at the demise. This sense of loss would be expressed by train enthusiasts, steam buffs and tourists in general, pining for a New Zealand steam-hauled service somewhere. Anywhere.

To many New Zealanders, it might as well have been

nowhere. Way down towards the bottom of the South Island in fact, on a barely surviving branch line, between two tiny rural Southland settlements. It seemed a romantic sentiment quite in keeping with the left-wing leanings of the Norman Kirk-led Labour government of the early 1970s, which, among other indulgences, bought into the commune movement by supporting the development of alternative settlements called Ohu in various backs-of-beyond. The Kingston Flyer seemed to come out of the same bag. Peter Gordon, Minister of Railways in the late 1960s and the General Manager of New Zealand Railways, Ivan Thomas, had a lot to do with officially floating the splendid notion of developing the modern Kingston Flyer concept. After meeting with locals at a public meeting in Lumsden to discuss aspects of closure of the line to Kingston, the idea of steam-hauled excursions on the line bubbled to the surface. When Ivan Thomas suggested a steam-hauled tourist train, the minister stirred even more.

'What a damned good idea,' enthused Peter Gordon. He was aware of one or two locomotives left 'lying around' after the demise of steam. They would be suitable for restoration. The idea that an old ministerial carriage, also surplus to requirements, be resurrected was apparently and appropriately the minister's too.

Such frivolity. The crazy concept, despite misgivings, gathered pace. The old, ornate Riversdale Station was relocated to Kingston, the line upgraded and engine and carriage restoration commenced.

The Labour government of the mid-1980s would have blanched at the notion of a 'toy' train being backed by the government, to trundle between Lumsden and Kingston on an old Southland branch line that had been losing money for years. But back in the days of the revival of the Kingston Flyer, market forces were largely foreign to us.

The inaugural run of the reconstituted Flyer on 21 December 1971 was a day of poignancy and celebration.

At Lumsden close to 5000 people were waiting for the train from Invercargill, which was double headed as it pulled into the new southern terminus. AB778 had the honour of hauling the first train from Lumsden north to Kingston on this famous day of resurrection. Russell Glendinning, at the time the only full-time steam loco operator employed by NZ Railways, began his stint as one of the more famous Kiwi engine drivers as he prepared the train for departure.

Meanwhile Lumsden throbbed with excitement. The inaugural run was a gala occasion. Floats formed a parade; traction engines steamed around the streets. Speeches were made, and a blue ribbon cut by Peter Gordon with the help of a 'local lass'.

At Kingston, pandemonium reigned. The station yard was packed with thousands of sightseers. Veteran cars added to the feeling of something venerable being revisited. Vintage displays were thronged with bystanders keen to soak up the ambience. A pipe band added to the aural montage as it piped the train into the station, and at one stage the skirl almost harmonised with the triumphant peel of the steam engine's whistle as it recreated an important part of Southland history.

The Kingston Flyer, the name, had a ring to it, although some conservative locals labelled it the Noddy train. At

Soon celebrities, MPs, Cabinet Ministers, Mayors, executives and press and TV folk took their places on the train, which chuffed away from Lumsden at 1.00pm.

a time when the Marrakesh Express was the train to be seen on (thanks to Crosby, Stills and Nash), the Flyer appealed to younger people as well as rail traditionalists and ordinary tourists. The fact that it didn't leave from a sizable centre of population may have been scoffed at by middle-of-the-roaders but added to its appeal to the counter-culture generation of the 70s. Its southern terminus could have been the city of Invercargill, but the central Southland town of Lumsden was chosen. The fact that Lumsden used to be called 'Elbow' only added to the new train's mystique.

This unlikely demographic took an interest in the revamped Flyer from the outset, swelling patronage in the early years. The Kingston Flyer was cool. Partly as a consequence the new train enjoyed encouraging profits for several years. The fact that it was the only remaining steam-hauled service on the national system added to its status and mystique. Indeed many steam freaks and tourists from other parts of the globe made regular

OPPOSITE Like a venerable grandfather, the 83-year-old AB engine of the Kingston Flyer provides a platform for an expectant young traveller.

pilgrimages to Southland to ride the Flyer. Such is the pulling power of steam.

In the 1970s the Kingston Flyer was deemed an instant success. The novelty factor may have had something to do with it, but there was also a genuine interest displayed by New Zealand holiday makers and overseas tourists. In its first month of operation the new train earned $23,000 and in the first few years averaged 29,000 passengers each summer season. It rapidly developed iconic status. A National Film Unit documentary, *A Train for Christmas*, starred the new tourist train. It quickly revived the era of the romantic rail journey.

It even developed a modern-day reputation for speed. When a man suffered a heart attack at the isolated Five Rivers settlement, the train was obliged to step on the gas to get the patient to Lumsden as soon as possible. The Kingston Flyer flew. Fourteen kms in 12 ¹/₂ minutes to be precise.

As it did in the old days, the Kingston Flyer linked with the Lake Wakatipu steamer *Earnslaw* for a while, but although this arrangement was not really successful, other launch operators stepped into the breach to transport passengers from Kingston to Queenstown.

For many years after its reintroduction in 1971 the Kingston Flyer and the Wakatipu steamers provided a goods service to Queenstown and the Lake Wakatipu district. It was just a matter of attaching wagons behind the green heritage carriages. While this service may have added a more utilitarian, less romantic aspect, it produced practical benefits.

The Kingston Flyer operation, in terms of motive force and rolling stock, consisted of two AB engines, seven vintage wooden carriages (seating capacity 226 passengers, with a total capacity of 320), a buffet car based on an old saloon carriage, a car-van and a 'birdcage' car that was once the ministerial carriage. On the back of such equipment the Flyer took off, but then faltered as patronage dwindled, politicians dithered and market forces intruded.

Climatic factors played a part in the life-cycle of the Kingston Flyer too. Away back in 1939 the original Flyer was thwarted by engulfing snow drifts north of Lumsden that saw the train stranded in the wilderness for a day or two. In 1979, at a time when the modern-day Flyer was beginning to feel the economic pinch, severe flooding led to the line between Mararoa Junction and Garston being washed out. New Zealand Rail decided not to repair the track and the link between Lumsden and Kingston was severed. For a while some of the romance died.

The service was tried on the Invercargill run for a time and soon interests outside Southland began making overtures about shifting the train to other, more populous regions of the country. Marlborough was one suggestion. There was even an ambitious notion to construct 11 km of new track on the Queenstown Hill where the Kingston Flyer would take diners on a circuit that overlooked the Shotover River, many metres below. It changed ownership several times. Some arrangements became complex as the powers-that-be realised the operation of a stand-alone railway presented special problems. For a time it became an orphan railway.

Despite such identity crises, the Flyer became well-

OPPOSITE Still flying after all these years. The Kingston Flyer above Lake Wakatipu.

The Kingston Flyer, Colin Meads, Taihape gumboots, Sir Edmund Hillary, the buzzy bee. I don't know where the Flyer ranks in an array of Kiwi icons, but it would be in my top 20.

known to many as the Crunchie Bar Special, based on an advertisement extolling the appeal of a famous Kiwi chocolate-coated novelty. The TV ad filmed on the train with actors dressed up as train robbers, while nanas continued knitting imperviously, became one of the iconic TV images of the 70s and 80s. But travelling on the Flyer with its ornate fixtures, pared-back wooden interiors and polished brass soon reminds you that the train has a real identity. It's a unique vintage experience, even if these days it only covers the 14 km to Fairlight before returning to Kingston on Lake Wakatipu. However, such is the power of advertising you still half expect to see renegades on horseback poised at every bend to attack the train, and mean hombres with smoking guns in the buffet.

At the time of writing in 2007 the Kingston Flyer is still running. That's the good news. From October to May it chuffs along at its own pace in its own space. On the stretch from Kingston to Fairlight it has no opposing traffic, not unless it is playing host to a special vintage rail event or

significant occasion. The Kingston Flyer experience remains a friendly, chortling gambol through remarkable country that still feels as if it's in the middle of nowhere.

I remember speaking to a Dunedin woman, an academic who had completed her thesis on the theme of excursion trains in the deep south. To celebrate her 50th birthday her family had hired the Kingston Flyer for a special surprise birthday run. The icing on her cake was an invitation to travel part of the way in the driver's cab.

It's a bit disquieting that it doesn't stretch out all the way to Lumsden in the South any more, but it's easy enough to get over that truncation. The shorter run is obviously easier to maintain and the service has become more accessible for special events and private charters. The Flyer is now involved in the type of tour package that reflects the growing sophistication of the tourism industry in New Zealand.

Twice a day the Flyer undertakes the round trip from Kingston to Fairlight, half an hour each way. It is now arguably the most remote passenger train in New Zealand. Since the demise of the Southerner, which carried passengers from Christchurch to Invercargill, Fairlight, a lonely yet alluring stopping point with little more than a railway station (installed in 1997 when the old Otautau Station further south was procured from Tranz Rail), represents one of the most southerly stations to see people stepping down from a train.

To begin at the beginning, the departure setting at Kingston is tranquil and picturesque. The waters of the lake lap in the near distance. Steep, bush-clad cliffs studded with rocky outcrops provide the immediate backdrop for the station and other rail-related buildings. The Flyer itself waits patiently, glinting in the sun.

The Kingston Flyer, Colin Meads, Taihape gumboots, Sir Edmund Hillary, the buzzy bee. I don't know where the Flyer ranks in an array of Kiwi icons, but it would be in my top 20. When you come upon the train for the first time it elicits the overwhelming sense of recognition associated with seeing a celebrity in the flesh.

'It's a little beaut isn't it, mate,' says the generously proportioned Australian standing next to me at the station.

'A bit like your Puffing Billy perhaps,' I reply, referring to the famous vintage steam train that runs through the hills not far from Melbourne.

'A more handsome train, mate. I'd have to say that.'

'Those ABs were always fine looking specimens.'

'What about the Wallabies? It's not just the All Blacks who cut a dash, mate.'

'The ABs are the type of engine used on the Kingston Flyer.'

The Australian grunts. He's bushy of beard, a bit woolly of thinking, gregarious if a little garrulous. He looks like he's stepped out of the Crunchie Bar ad himself. A 28-km round trip seems a little tight in terms of getting to know a fellow traveller, but by the time we arrive back in Kingston, it feels as if I've known him for a while. Aussies can be like that.

I can call him Gav. His mother still calls him Gavin. I don't want to know what his father calls him, apparently. He is from a small mining settlement in South Australia. Broken Ring, or something. Not a million miles from Port Augusta. Not a hundred either. He speaks so quickly I'm not always able to keep up. We get on to cricket as we wait for the Kingston Flyer to depart.

'The trouble with the Black Caps, mate, is they've got no batsmen, mate. No bowlers either to speak of.'

'They've got a wicket-keeper though.'

'Yeah, but they're afraid of taking risks.' Bowling underarm is a risky business but I decide not to mention the 1981 controversy. It's like not mentioning the war to Germans. Besides, it's time to concentrate on the journey ahead and take stock of the motive force.

Engine number AB778 is immaculately turned out. Ribbons of brass, white wheel rims and flashes of red complement its shiny black presence. It is one of two ABs restored for pulling purposes. The other, AB795, was converted from a former WAB engine, whereas 778 was always a purebred AB. Built in 1925 it is now over 80 years old but doesn't look a day over 20. AB795, originally built in 1927, was converted to AB status in 1947, the year I was born. Given my affinity with steam engines (encountering a K at Te Kuiti Station was one of my earliest memories), such a coincidence strikes me as being in some way profound. More important, the AB has been described as the most popular and efficient all-round locomotive to have steamed in New Zealand. And it was a home-grown product.

The green of the heritage carriages is distinguished, the gold trim a nice finishing touch. It is essentially the Pullman green widely used by NZ Rail until the mid 1920s. Our train also includes the car-van, a vehicle that is a regulation carriage with a luggage and guards' compartment occupying one end. There is also the bird-cage car that features a balcony running along one side, defined by a wire mesh wall, which affords passengers the chance to view the great outdoors and feel the keening breeze. And build up an appetite that can be satisfied in the old saloon car buffet.

If the Kingston Flyer did little more than remain static at Kingston Station, it would have served its purpose. As a rail museum piece and work of art it is worth the price of admission alone. But we get to travel on this moving exhibit.

The Kingston Flyer, right on schedule, eases away from its home base near the lake's edge, leaving behind the coal-loading facilities, water tower, turntable, loco shed and workshops. The line heads south, rising and curving steadily. AB778 works efficiently, climbing up through the glacial moraine, past an old quarry and several farms before easing out across an isolated desert-like stretch, with the Hector Mountains to the east and Eyre Mountains to the west. At 365 metres the line reaches its highest point, but you're scarcely aware of the elevation as the train opens out along the straight leading to Fairlight. The highway has already left the line to its own devices, a common enough situation with New Zealand railways.

Yoko, an attractive young Japanese woman, proves to be an interesting travelling companion. She is a student from Kobe and a genuine aficionado of train travel. The Kingston Flyer is her final rail journey after starting out on the Overlander in Auckland two weeks earlier. Not only does she revere train travel, she puts train drivers on a pedestal. To her they are on a par with pop stars. She has collected scores of autographs of train staff in general and drivers in particular. She shows me a photo of the driver of the TranzAlpine signing her book at Arthur's Pass.

As the Kingston Flyer stretches out along the Fairlight Flat she expresses her disappointment that there is no train to Milford Sound, although she takes delight in the steam-hauled excursion that is now billowing and blustering its way southward. Although there is no train to Milford Sound and Fiordland, we are able to compare notes about a train that did descend to the base of a fiord — the Myrdal to Flam rack-rail service in Norway that dropped dramatically, threading its way beneath waterfalls and tip-toeing along a rock shelf before pulling into one of the most remote and remarkable railway stations in the world. Both of us have travelled that precipitous track and I am able to assure Yoko that I will do everything in my power to cajole the authorities into cutting a similar line through to Milford Sound, extending the line from Kingston to Queenstown then on through Glenorchy and via the Homer Tunnel.

Such musings are not mine alone. Back in the 1880s the government was asked to consider building a line from Kingston to Queenstown and back eastwards to Cromwell. When it was ascertained that such a route would generate little revenue-earning capacity between Kingston and Frankton, through having to compete with cheaper freight cartage provided by the Lake Wakatipu steam-boats, the idea was dismissed by the Royal Commission on Railways. Another proposal offered up the spectre of a railway line from Lake Wakatipu to a port on Lake McKerrow, near Martin's Bay, which opened out, via the Hollyford River, on to the West Coast of the South Island. That notion was similarly scotched. It might have made more sense to go for a line to Milford Sound. As the crow flies it's closer.

Thanks to some preparatory research I am able to tell Yoko about aspects of the early history of the line, over a portion of which the Kingston Flyer was showing its true colours. I tell her about the wooden rails. As these rapidly disintegrated, there were tales of passengers being asked to leave their comfort zone in the carriages and help push the train. And they were still obliged to pay. At one stage the trains became horse-drawn when it was concluded that locomotives were too heavy and caused too much damage. Once an irate woman passenger got off the train, not to lend her delicate weight to proceedings, but to walk towards her destination beside the wooden rails. She explained that she was in a hurry and walking pace was better than the horse-drawn apparition could manage. Inevitably, conventional railway lines were laid and the horses put out to pasture.

The Kingston Flyer has by now drifted into Fairlight, snuggled up to the old Otautau Station, and is preparing to return to Kingston. I have to say I don't recall much of the turnaround. Yoko continues to talk as we climb down on to the platform, although the magnificent domes of the Hector Mountains silence me. This is scenery, flecked with early winter snow, that demands contemplation, and it's fine by me if Yoko continues to express her delight, without a contribution from me.

Now we are away again, heading north. The return journey is a time of contemplation. Even Yoko has run

out of words. The scenery is tranquillising. It's like being part of a landscape painted in water colours. Some of the hues of Central Otago have made it this far south. There's certainly something about the isolation that brings its own comfort.

The grass is short and muted yellow up here. It's a definite plateau and you feel reassured by that for some reason. No wild undulations and blind corners. Plateaux

A train for young and old. Flyer passengers enter into the spirit of a unique train ride.

have a permanence about them. We could talk about big skies, and we have, but size doesn't always matter. The sky on the Fairlight straight is big enough but its more the sense of enclosure that leaves you feeling secure. Montana's sky was monstrous. Yoko and I both agree on that, but at times you felt lost, even on a train like Amtrak's Empire Builder. Horizons melted, mild agoraphobia set in. The sense of vastness left you pining for a valley or a mountain range.

Up here on the way back to Kingston, there are mountains on either side. The snow sparkles on the upper reaches. A series of foothills angle back on one another, creating a layered effect. The remoteness is profound. You try to imagine human settlements up in the folds of the land, but you can't. That's one of the majestic features of the central areas of the South Island, the loneliness of the land. But for this railway, and even then it's only a short stretch, the plains around Fairlight would seem untouched. It could be Patagonia, but why hanker after that when New Zealand has this?

One day, new settlers may make this quiet stretch their home. The new southward migration that has seen Queenstown and Arrowtown and other central locations become the home of new migrants from the gridlocked north, will inevitably reach this far south. Lodges and huge holiday homes of variable character will probably appear. Mind you, it would be a matchless place to live. Etched into the side of a Fairlight foothill, burnt-out city slickers may look down on the muted yellow plains as the daily Kingston Flyer services belch white coal smoke into the keening air. Such emissions,

rather than creating environmental concerns, will be seen to be at one with this hidden wilderness. Unless too many northerners invade these pristine reaches and emissions of all kinds become noxious. Perhaps that's one of the unspoken reasons why the Kingston Flyer has been let loose along this remote stretch. As yet there are no objectionable aspects to its passage.

Coming off the plateau and drifting and curving down towards the lake's edge brings a feeling of disappointment. Just when you're becoming totally absorbed by the scenery, the chuffing of the AB and friendly sway of the carriages, it begins to come to an end.

As the Flyer rounds the final curve and cruises elegantly to a stop at the Kingston platform, you feel you'd give your right arm to make the journey again. As I say sayonara to Yoko, I realise I won't have to give my right arm. There is another out and back journey from Kingston to Fairlight, leaving in two hours. In a state of mild euphoria I wander around Kingston town. At a leisurely pace I take in the ornate station and souvenir shop, visit the Kingston Flyer Tavern Café and soak up some of the local atmosphere.

If I find myself totally hooked on the Kingston Flyer experience, even after the afternoon's service, it's comforting to know I can bunk down indefinitely in the Kingston Motels and Holiday Park. Between trains, if I'm at a loose end, there are BBQ and recreational areas, walking tracks, a nine-hole golf course and bowling green to while away the time until the whistle blasts. I can even cast a line into the lake's waters, live off the land a bit.

Of course life goes on, as does that of the Kingston Flyer. Yet it's a little unsettling once I've returned home to

OPPOSITE The pulling power of steam. The AB motive force propels the Flyer across the Fairlight Flat.

come across an article in a rail magazine that attests to the on-going complexity of the Kingston Flyer's ownership and future.

In March 2005 an Auckland-based property developer, Investors Forum, bought the Kingston Flyer, box and dice — or most of it. The transaction included the land and tracks owned by Kingston Flyer Steam Train Limited and the two steam locos and all the passenger carriages that had been secured by an outfit called Invest South in 2002. The latter had purchased the rolling stock from Tranz Rail with the view of retaining the train in Southland and in public ownership.

A certain level of paranoia surrounds the investment and development plans of the new owners. Some cynics have suggested the train might be endangered by the intention to develop the lakefront and other pockets of Kingston. Cynics like me can at least feel reassured that the Kingston Flyer is still flying a year on from the change of ownership and, apparently, direction.

The resurrection and survival of the modern era Kingston Flyer, once described as the Noddy Train that left originally from Lumsden (formerly Elbow and latterly 'Petticoat Junction'), has been a triumph. The contribution made by senior train driver Russell Glendinning to the train's development and profile was rewarded with the British Empire Medal for services to tourism in Southland. Yoko's elevation of train drivers to the status of rock stars seems to assume a certain credibility thanks to Glendinning's belief in the Kingston Flyer and his subsequent decoration.

Archaeologically speaking, the Kingston Flyer's past has developed a sort of cult status too. On the banks of the Oreti River, further back down the old line, one of the original Flyer engines, K88, was relieved of its duties shoring up the river bank, resurrected and made over. It now spends its days steaming happily along the tracks of the Plains Railway in Mid-Canterbury and on one famous occasion it returned to its original stamping ground on the Kingston Flyer route.

You have to wonder if such a relic would have been disturbed if the Kingston Flyer had not taken wing in 1971.

Between Christmas 1971 and Easter 1979 the Flyer registered more than 231 passenger journeys with a full house of 300 travellers. It would be interesting to know the number chalked up in the last 27 years. Some of the rides would be credited to the rail pilgrim from Western Australia who, on an annual basis, travels to New Zealand exclusively to ride the Kingston Flyer. But most of them would be first-time travellers, international and local, largely unaware that this short journey would turn out to be such a jewel in the crown of New Zealand train travel.

② MIDDLEMARCH IN THE MIDDLE OF APRIL
THE TAIERI GORGE RAILWAY

MIDDLEMARCH

Sutton

Mount Stoker

Pukerangi

Hindon

Christmas Creek

Wingatui

Otago Harbour

DUNEDIN

Beyond Kingston and the Kingston Flyer there is no connecting train to Dunedin, just a rumbling bus through the bleak, beautiful Central Otago landscape, redolent of Grahame Sydney paintings and Brian Turner tone-poems.

Dunedin Railway Station — perhaps New Zealand's finest.

PREVIOUS PAGE The 'Moonscape Express'. The Taieri Gorge Limited in its element.

Back in the 1970s it was possible to bunk down in a stone-walled bed and breakfast establishment at Alexandra and catch the NZR railcar service in the early morning to Dunedin. In earlier days you could spend even less time on the bus or service car and catch a steam-hauled connection from Cromwell that chuffed through the lunar landscapes and small country towns like Clyde, Alexandra and Ranfurly (time for refreshments), before descending through the schist formations of the Taieri Gorge and merging with the main south line at Wingatui Junction. After a bit of a shuffle of wagons and a farewell to passengers due to head further south to Invercargill, the AB-hauled mixed goods would head north past Caversham and Carisbrook into Dunedin Station.

When I first came to Dunedin back in the 1960s its distinctive Victorian and Edwardian buildings, its old villas and churches, and the friendliness of the locals left an indelible impression. With its well-established university and student culture and obvious love of the arts and literature (there's a statue of Scottish poet Robert Burns in the Octagon, Dunedin's heart), it was a stimulating place to be. Dunedin and Dunedinites felt settled, established. There was a sense of history. Original buildings remained, whereas in the North Island they would have been bowled in the name of progress.

Even the students of Dunedin seemed more settled and at one with the charm and history of New Zealand's first city of influence. A hundred years earlier Dunedin had become the first financial centre of New Zealand on the back of the discovery of gold in the hinterland. It became a city of firsts, the setting for the country's first university, medical school, daily newspaper and electric trams and cable cars.

Appropriately, I first arrived in the city by train. The railway, unlike the central North Island where the Main Trunk was not completed until 1908, was up and running in Dunedin in the 1870s. The line south was one of the first links under the Vogel Public Works scheme. It was the first major line to be built to the new uniform gauge of 1067 mm — 3'6". The initial section to the suburb of Abbotsford was opened in 1874 and in September of the following year the line reached Balclutha in the south. Considering that construction workers had to bore through the 890–m Chain Hills tunnel between Abbotsford and Wingatui, such progress was seen to be dramatic. Meanwhile the line north of Dunedin reached Christchurch in 1878.

Within the city limits of Dunedin too, rail construction was progressing apace. The Port Chalmers branch to the main port of Dunedin was the first line of any kind in New Zealand to be constructed using the new 1067-mm gauge. Soon Dunedinites were commuting down the branch. Nearly 140 years later, one of the latest and more successful rail ventures is the Taieri Gorge Railway. Tourists from visiting cruise liners begin their journeys from Port Chalmers, setting out for a ride up the Taieri Gorge.

In 1876 the Dunedin Peninsula and Ocean Beach Railway began operating on a 3.5–km line to Ocean Beach and, at the end of 1877, another 1.5–km branch to Anderson's Bay signalled further early expansion. Although the Ocean Beach line operated primarily as a steam tramway, from 1880 trains still carried passengers to race meetings at Forbury Park racecourse. Such race services and trains to agricultural shows ran until 1904, several years before the North Island main trunk was completed and, even after passenger services dwindled, the line was used for four-legged passengers — livestock being transported to and from shows — until 1938.

These days the Ocean Beach Railway still operates in a vintage capacity. Again this tourist attraction is a first. When the Otago Railway and Locomotive Society began running the Ocean Beach Railway in 1961, it was the first operating museum railway in the country. Weather permitting, it swings into action every Sunday between November and June in Kettle Park, St Kilda, near the original Ocean Beach railway terminus.

Not surprisingly, the city has a fascination with trains. New Zealand's first steam engine to be commissioned for work on the 1067–mm standard gauge — a Fairlie — can be found in a glass case beside the Otago Settlers Museum. Fittingly the museum also showcases JA1274, the last Dunedin-built steam engine to work on the South Island main trunk between Christchurch and Invercargill, via Dunedin.

Much of Dunedin's fondness for trains derives from the fact that the Hillside workshops located in the southern suburbs on the TGR route to the Gorge saw the construction, maintenance and conversion of many locomotives and a great deal of general rolling stock over the years. Despite the threat of closure, the works are now heavily involved in the upgrading of additional passenger carriages for expanding suburban and inter-city services and other specialised rolling stock.

Excursion trains through the Taieri Gorge are not new. Back in the 1960s there was a certain cachet attached to the Blossom Festival excursions that travelled up to Alexandra to help celebrate the ripening of the local bounty — apricots mainly but other fruit of the vine as well — that provided Dunedinites with a reason to kick up their heels.

The Otago branch of the New Zealand Railway and Locomotive Society had been running diesel-hauled forays since the demise of steam in 1968 and the level of public interest was high from the outset. The Taieri Gorge

Railway had its genesis in the Otago Excursion Train Trust, which was formed in 1979, at a time when New Zealand Rail was kyboshing carriages right and left. So the OETT began operating its own carriages with New Zealand Rail engines providing the motive force.

It seemed a logical progression when the OETT inaugurated the Taieri Gorge Limited in 1987, a summer season fling that saw daily trains run to and from Pukerangi. When the government decided to close the Central Otago line in 1990 the Dunedin City Council came to the party, buying the track to Middlemarch, all relevant fixed equipment and five DJ locos. As part of the deal the community was obliged to raise $1 million to help finance the project.

These days ownership of the Taieri Gorge Railway is split between the Dunedin City Council (72%) and the OETT (28%). When you find yourself being drawn in by the mesmerising scenery of the Taieri Gorge a sense of horror descends as you realise this splendid railway experience could have been wiped out with the stroke of a bureaucrat's pen. You tip your hat to the good folk of Otago for raising what turned out to be $1.2 million, ensuring that the Taieri Gorge Railway would become New Zealand's longest private railway and perhaps its most scenic.

The offices of the TGR are located in the stately old Dunedin railway station. Half an hour before the Dunedin to Middlemarch train is due to leave, the place is buzzing. Ticket sales are transacted, seat and carriage numbers allocated and brochures uplifted. Kids can scarcely contain themselves. Of course negotiating Dunedin station is in itself part of the appeal of travelling on what is one of New Zealand's best-loved tourist attractions.

The station is dazzling inside and out. It has a 37-metre-high clock tower for a start, and a stunning façade. The facings and ornamental work were made from Oamaru limestone. The main body of the structure, designed and built by Sir George Troup, was made of stone transported in from Hyde, Central Otago. It is perhaps New Zealand's most impressive railway station, although someone once described it as an elongated chocolate cake with white icing droplets. Built in the Flemish Renaissance style, it has also been described as the finest Edwardian structure in New Zealand. Indeed, the finest stone structure altogether. George Troup won his knighthood on the strength of it and the nickname Gingerbread George.

The entrance hall features a distinctive mosaic floor made by Royal Doulton. Rail scenes are illustrated on the hundreds of thousands of porcelain squares. Across the floor the busy staff members of the Taieri Gorge Railway ensure all passengers are accounted for. With the phasing out of the Southerner passenger service, the TGR has sole use of the conventional aspects of the station, although a restaurant has found its way into a ground floor enclave. On the first floor of the station is the New Zealand Sports Hall of Fame. Priceless Kiwi artefacts like the armguard that All Black Colin Meads, one of New Zealand's most famous rugby players, used while playing two test matches against South Africa with a broken arm, can be viewed here.

Towards the end of 2006 the centenary of the station was celebrated. Labour Weekend that year saw a steam excursion from Picton to Dunedin bring hundreds of

OPPOSITE Worth the price of admission alone — the ornate interior of Dunedin Station.

The way our grandparents used to travel. The interior of a TGR heritage carriage.

services. He has been visiting family in Oamaru and sees no reason why he can't make it to Dunedin to travel on both the Dunedin to Middlemarch train and the following day's Seasider to Palmerston.

After being allocated seats we go looking for the train. A consist made up of at least ten carriages, two DJ engines and a smaller DE occupies the main platform. All the carriages are of the heritage style, dating back to the 1920s, with traditional sash windows and wooden trim. The modern panorama carriages with sweeping windows and air conditioning are conspicuous by their absence. We figure our consist is a more rustic and authentic set and do not grieve over the issue. The distinctive yellow and brown livery gives the carriages a beacon-like focus in the morning gloom.

I note that the motive force is made up of DJ3211, DJ3286 and DE1337. I don't normally take too much notice of such details and figure I am suffering from a mild form of trainspotting. I also get quite a start when another engine attached to a shorter train, made up of a combination of heritage and panorama cars, coughs into life behind me at the dock platform to the south of the station.

Could that be our train, given that it is showing earlier signs of life than the three-engined monster facing south? The friendly TGR staff confirm that, no, that isn't our train behind the now smoothly throbbing single engine in the dock platform and, yes, that is the train to Middlemarch on the main platform. It too will soon be spluttering into action. On cue our motive force emits its initial roar, alerting travellers of the need to take their seats. An elderly couple, drawn by the earlier ignition of the

celebrants into the city. Steam trains also ran on the TGR line up to Middlemarch and back. The old southern route to Invercargill carried passenger trains for the first time in many years. Steam train shuttles to and from Sawyers Bay, a few kilometres north of the city, and trains to Hillside complemented the smorgasbord of celebratory rail activity.

Earlier in 2000, after several years of faithful and expensive restoration, Dunedin station's modern-day makeover was complete. It stands as one of the wonders of New Zealand railways.

Russell, an old mate, is along for the ride on the TGR

single engine are now climbing sheepishly down from the wrong train and taking their place in our carriage, which happens to be car E. Almost immediately the diesels roar and we are sliding out of George Troup's matchless station and plunging into the suburbs of south Dunedin.

The line threads its way through the older suburbs of South Dunedin, past the Hillside Railway Workshops, lying in a depression below the line. The first 12 km of the journey follows the course of the South Island Main Trunk. The TGR Limited, as it is often labelled, is currently the only passenger service to touch the old, sacred stretch between Dunedin and Invercargill in the deep south. Green Island and Abbotsford, the site of a disastrous landslide, eases by. In 1979, after a number of warning signs, a massive slip destroyed or rendered uninhabitable 69 homes. Six hundred and forty local residents were evacuated. Amazingly there were no deaths or serious injuries as the hillside collapsed.

The woman sitting across the aisle from us is keen to point out to her friend the whereabouts of Green Island. It's always fascinated me, Green Island, and how it got its name. It's not so much green as suburban grey and it's not exactly surrounded by water. Perhaps there was a flood when they were handing out names. The woman and her friend, along with their respective husbands, are from Nelson and this is their first time on the TGR too.

At Wingatui Junction the train pulls into the faithfully renovated, New Zealand Historic Places Trust registration '2' station. Several passengers get on here. Suddenly the TGR train seems like an old-world stopping service. Wingatui, the name, sounds like an authentic Maori word. However, this is not the case. Many years ago a pakeha shooter, out with his gun, winged a tui in a brazen and nowadays politically incorrect act on the site of Wingatui.

Wingatui Junction is 34 m above sea level, which is not a lot, but it is a start — in more ways than one. The Otago Central Railway, or what's left of it, veers north-west from here leaving the main trunk behind. We are now on the Taieri Plains, scene of the crippling 1980 floods that saw the nearby Dunedin Airport at Momona awash and out of commission for some time. Three days after our traverse, the heavens were to open up again and floodwaters cover large tracts of the plains. In a remarkable vignette a pet goldfish would be located a long way from home, where it had been spirited by the swirling waters, and as the TV cameras whirred, it would be returned to its home base.

Wingatui Racecourse comes and goes. Not a horse in sight. Nor an aeroplane, although Russ, a pilot and owner of a small plane, half expected to be able to see his plane on the plains as we passed the perimeter of Taieri Aerodrome. The on-board commentary is now on full throttle and we soon become aware of the Fisher and Paykel whiteware factory off to the left and south.

The line climbs above the Taieri Plains. Construction began at Wingatui on this section of the Central Otago link back in 1879. Its slow progress was typical of the drawn-out nature of much New Zealand rail development, with the depression of the 1880s preventing its extension beyond Hindon in the middle of the Taieri Gorge even by 1889. Middlemarch was eventually reached in 1891. The Central Otago route was chosen in 1877 because it

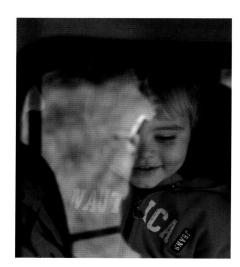

The excitement of kids and train travel seem to go together.

OPPOSITE Saying goodbye to the Main South Line. Wingatui Junction where the Taieri Gorge Railway tracks actually begin.

opened up the largest expanse of Crown lands and proved to be the most direct passage to Dunedin. By the mid-1870s Otago's gold rushes were a distant memory and the agricultural and pastoral potential of the central regions drove the perceived need for railway construction.

As the train continues climbing through Salisbury Tunnel it's interesting to contemplate the notion that the course of the railway was selected from seven alternatives, because this was also the least challenging from an engineering perspective. Did that mean the Taieri Gorge was not all it was cracked up to be? The least challenging route for the line might mean the spectacular scenery depicted in the photos and brochures was an illusion, achieved with mirrors or enhanced computer graphics.

Some hope. Beyond Salisbury Tunnel, the longest on the line at 437 m, the Wingatui Viaduct announces the beginning of the 'least challenging' route. Many passengers make for the viewing platforms at each end of the heritage carriages, their cameras cocked. The viaduct, 197 m long and 47 m above Mullocky Stream, is the largest wrought iron structure in the southern hemisphere. The question is, which is the largest wrought iron structure in the northern hemisphere?

'Eiffel Tower', one of the Nelson men announces as he joins the stampede to the exterior of the train. It's the first time he has spoken. I guess he's right about the Eiffel Tower. Is there a French person on board to confirm the claim? There probably is, given that we have already detected a healthy proportion of foreign tourists.

There's something decidedly different and appealing about the bridges and viaducts along the Taieri Gorge route. Admittedly the Wingatui viaduct does not feature the ornate stone columns that characterise most of them. Just all that wrought iron that lends it the appearance of the viaducts associated with the North Island Main Trunk. But its approach is dramatic as you emerge from the Mullocky tunnel before edging over what turns out to be the largest structure on the line.

Soon we encounter the Taieri River off to the left. Russ grumbles about being stuck on the wrong side of the train, with all the unfolding scenery and dramas apparently concentrated out the window closest to the Nelsonians' seats. We jump around like ill-trained dogs trying to catch a glimpse of the gorge before joining the knot of passengers standing outside on the windswept viewing platform.

At a place, or what was once a place, called Parera, some 16 km from the turn-off at Wingatui, we pass the old railway house that used to be associated with a crossing station. The house is now a holiday home, complete with very little it seems. No power, no phone, no TV, no road access, just woodburning fires and stoves and wet backs, and a splendid sense of isolation and natural beauty.

'A bit of a one-house town,' the tall Nelson man bellows above the clatter of carriage wheels and the rising wind. A flock of ducks swirl in the eddying river waters below the house. Parera is the Maori name for the grey duck. I'd imagine the ducks would be good company if you found yourself stranded up here at the mouth of the gorge. Someone to talk to as the rocky walls closed in. Duck Point Tunnel, back down the tracks, attests to the high status of ducks along this lonely stretch.

Mount Allan is the next stop, not that the train stops here on the TGR service, although many years ago there used to be a station that served a sheep run with no road access. That used to be one of the more remarkable aspects of the former New Zealand Rail service — but for the trains, this neck of the woods would have been inaccessible. To us it was the dark side of the moon, and that was before the lunar landscapes further along the track entered the picture. And for a significant swathe of the eastern hills before the gorge closes in, this is a real neck of the woods — pine plantations in fact.

A modern rail tale is emerging too. The Mount Allan sheep operation was converted to forestry 20 years ago. The trees will soon be ready for chopping and transporting to Port Chalmers. The TGR is ideally placed to provide cartage by rail. According to recent reports TGR have in fact tendered for the right to run two log trains a day on their revamped passenger route. There's some sort of irony in this although I'm too peckish and caffeine-deprived to unravel it at ten o'clock in the morning.

Steam engines used to quench their thirsts at Little Mount Allan. We do the same. Russ tries a cup of Twinings English breakfast tea. I stick to coffee. The muffins stick to our ribs like all good muffins should.

At Christmas Creek some of our Christmases come at once. After we've resigned ourselves to being located on the unlucky side of the train, the line suddenly arches away to the west on the Christmas Creek viaduct and we remain alert enough to realise we are now staring into the mouth of the ravine from our side of the train. And the gorge seemed to be getting deeper, the schist rock

formations more ornate and other-worldly. Grey and columnated, they often take on a manmade appearance. Condominiums for rabbits. Often pancaked and oblong, but more often randomly hewn and strewn by the ravages of time.

The Nelsonians are now mincing around our enclosure, aware that the balance of spectator power has shifted to our side of the train. The Taieri Gorge is getting more and more momentous.

Twenty-seven km out from Wingatui and at 71 m above sea level we come to a stop at Hindon. I remember stories about kids going to school by jigger around here. What a way to get to a place you really didn't want to be. Hindon is still a crossing station although nothing crosses us as we prepare to alight to soak up the remoteness and wild beauty.

Excellent rail journeys bring out the best in people. Nola from Nelson chats away as we climb down at Hindon and absorb the spectacular surroundings. She offers to take a photo of us, which produces a nice shot of Russ and me against the bright yellow background of our TGR carriage among all that grey schist. She won't hear of us taking a photo of her in the same circumstances, but we manage an on-board shot as the train begins to move deeper into the mysterious gorge, fording gulches and viaducts that have special significance for her.

Nola's grandmother lived at an outpost called Omakau. Her father, Nola's great-grandfather, toiled away on the construction of this wondrous railway from Dunedin to Cromwell. Omakau is located on a section of the old line

OPPOSITE Parera, the 'one-house town', near the beginning of the gorge.

that no longer exists. Not unless you count the Rail Trail circuit that sees trampers and cyclists retracing the steps of her great-grandfather all those years ago.

After crossing Pay Office Creek, Machine Creek and Deep Stream, which in fact seems quite shallow from way up here where the TGR clings like fingernails to the cliff face, and by plunging through Machine Creek tunnel and Deep Stream tunnel, we are able to proceed through this magnificent wilderness. Beyond Deep Stream we begin to climb dramatically higher.

'It's grand, just like the Rio Grande,' the taller of the Nelson men reckons as we cross Flat Stream, which did seem a bit flat, before disappearing into the Flat Stream tunnel.

'Have you done the Rio Grande Railway?' Russ asks.

'Done that, been there.'

The highest level, on this magical day in April, 2007, is Pukerangi. That isn't far up the line. The journey has been one big climb, from Wingatui on the plains to Pukerangi, the 'Hill of Heaven' at 250 m above sea level. All that's left, sadly, on this wondrous climb, is the Reefs, which features the 'Reefs Hotel', a tiny railway-red shack — more brown, really — beside the track, backing on to the upper reaches of the gorge.

You sense the dream run is coming to an end. As if to confirm it, the line leaves the Taieri River behind. At the time it seems like a permanent rupture of the relationship that has developed between the passengers and the river. We pull into Pukerangi. Most TGR trains end their journey here, but by judicious juggling of itineraries our train will soon head out over the Strath Taieri Plain towards Middlemarch, with the Rock and Pillar Range looming in the west.

Pukerangi is described as an historic small tablet station and has a 'Finest Survivor' categorisation from the Rail Heritage Trust. Full restoration of the station is on the cards. It was built in 1891 and developed in 1902 to encompass a post office. Its cream with red trim colour scheme makes it stand out against the dim hues of the surrounding Central Otago hinterland.

Some 10 km south of Middlemarch, the Matarae road-rail bridge carries the train towards the terminus. The PA system reminds us that this is one of only six such bridges surviving in New Zealand. Two are near Reefton on the West Coast of the South Island, another two between Greymouth and Hokitika further down the West Coast, and the other is at Pekatahi in the Bay of Plenty in the North Island.

Middlemarch was first reached by rail construction gangs in 1891. We arrive at lunch time, 2007. As you climb down from the train the flatness of the immediate terrain is in sharp contrast to the topsy-turvy gorge. Despite the Rock and Pillar Range, there's a 'big sky' feel to the landscape. Middlemarch is a quaint stopping post. Most of the 250 locals seem to be prodding the sausage sizzle into action on the platform or taking up their positions in the hotel directly opposite.

The Middlemarch railway house, listed as rail fan accommodation, is the old stationmaster's residence dating from the 1890s, made over to provide digs for up to eight travellers. It comes with all the amenities and is just across the road from the pub, where evening meals

The author and travelling companion stretch their legs.

OPPOSITE Curving around the Flat Stream Viaduct.

are provided. It would be a splendid base for unravelling the mystery of the Otago Central Rail Trail and we chalk it up for future reference.

A one-hour stopover provides the chance to take the Potted History Bus Tour, which meanders around the hinterland and deposits you at Sutton, back down the track, in time to catch the return service. There's also a craft shop, a museum and general store, not to mention the Kissing Gate Café, Blind Billy's Holiday Camp, the Police Station on Nottage Street, and a 10-minute walk, each way, to the cemetery.

The starkness of the landscape hits you as you wander across the road towards the hotel. The Rock and Pillars look close enough to climb. Then again, you imagine the embarrassment as the diesels bark out their departure clarion call and you are still only half-way up the eastern face. We make a mental note of the Rock and Pillars for future reference too.

I've gone out of my way to ensure that we travel on the TGR train that goes all the way to Middlemarch. The more common connection — indeed it runs every day of the year except Christmas Day — travels from Dunedin to Pukerangi. But I'm greedy. I want that extra 10 miles or so to Middlemarch, and still bemoan the fact that I am unable to go all the way to Alexandra as in the old days.

So we are having lunch at the Middlemarch pub — the Strath Taieri to be exact. It's an interesting intermingling of Scottish and Maori, the Strath Taieri. The hotel also provides an interesting intermingling of tourists, backpackers and locals.

Ben, a truck driver from Moonlight, out near MacRaes,

location of the largest gold mine in New Zealand, is one of the jovial locals who rub shoulders with us refugees off the train. He's busy with a mixed grill lunch at the time but that doesn't stop him making us feel at home in the Strath Taieri hotel. He speaks of the shot in the arm the TGR trains have provided for local spirits — and pockets. It's not just the regular tourist services either. Ben talks about the trainloads of single women from Dunedin who arrive in town on a bi-annual basis for a bit of dancing and cavorting, in the interests of relieving local single blokes of their frontier loneliness. Ben can't put a figure on it but he reckons several long-term unions have developed as a result. Locally they call the service 'The Love Train', with TGR carriages full of single women destined for the hijinks at the Middlemarch Singles Ball. In 2007 the train is still running.

After a certain amount of prodding I tell Ben that I'm gathering information for a book on New Zealand rail journeys. My jaunt on the TGR to Middlemarch is both business and pleasure. Whereupon Ben, an unassuming character, refers to me as Paul Theroux, the writer responsible for several books on rail journeys, and mentions that writer Brian Turner, brother of Glenn and Greg, brother-in-law of Sukhi Turner, the former long-serving Dunedin Mayor, lives deeper in the Central Otago recesses at a place called Oturehua. There he writes his robust poems and fleshes out biographies of iconic All Blacks like Colin Meads and Anton Oliver. If we take the Rail Trail we'll probably find him pecking away at his laptop.

Ben, an avowed rail fan although he drives a truck, is also a lover of literature. His favourite book, *All that blue*

OPPOSITE The stark beauty of the Strath Taieri Plains as the train approaches Pukerangi.

Pukerangi, a humble station at the highest point on the line. Most TGR services terminate here.

Otago truck driver from around these parts. Ben, despite his love of literature, is also a rugby follower and he seems saddened that McDonnell can no longer make it into the All Blacks.

'Don't forget to mention that Middlemarch Station is the oldest still in use in the South Island. It was built in 1873 during the Vogel era.' Ben's parting comment is that of a young man of many parts. We can't help wondering if he has been one of the benefactors of the 'Girls night out' special train.

'The Central Otago Rail Trail starts here too, Theroux,' he adds.

'Do you realise, Ben, that we've been to Middlemarch in the middle of March?'

'Good line Theroux, but it's actually the middle of April.'

While we're milling about on the platform my thoughts turn to the Rail Trail. Next time we'll have a go at it, perhaps on horseback, more likely bike-borne or on foot. We'll have to get some training in though. Training for a venture that used to feature trains. And Russ will have to be sporting an Achilles heel that isn't his Achilles heel. His recent operation has gone well but he's still hobbling.

In early March 2006, cyclists popped up everywhere along the Rail Trail like Central Otago rabbits. This is a new development. January is usually the most popular month but the burgeoning appeal into autumn is a local talking point. Spectacular autumn colours and the mildness of the weather, particularly in the middle of the day, have seen the gradual extension of the trail's season. A lot of 'Rail Trailers' set off from Clyde, but our train

can be, is a slim volume of poems put out by Brian Turner several years ago. That and *Tall Half-backs*, an account of growing up in the 1960s by a North Island author who at that stage published through John McIndoe Ltd., a Dunedin publishing house.

I don't know if it's kiwi reticence, fear of the tall poppy factor and a souring of relationships in the warm, friendly Middlemarch pub, but I feel it best to conceal the fact that I wrote *Tall Half-backs*. The latter had a lot of rail references, a theme Ben obviously identified with.

Joe McDonnell, a recent All Black, was a Central

today has provided a fair share from the Middlemarch commencement point.

The restoration of the Central Otago Rail Trail has seen developments like the preservation of Ranfurly Station, complete with two short lines of track, semaphore signals and the body of an old diesel engine, DJ3021, retained outside the station building. Clyde station is faithfully restored too.

At Wedderburn, the old goods shed has been transported back to its original site, after serving time as a curling club, and the station reinstated. In places the Rail Trail operates as an interactive museum. Trampers and cyclists and sundry riders relive the pioneering explorations of rail surveyors and construction gangs as they retrace the course of one of New Zealand's most scenic and legendary railway lines.

It's a strange old world. Although the tracks have been torn up beyond Middlemarch, it's heartening to see younger people with pedal power and sensible shoes defying the power of market forces and travelling along the embankments, through the tunnels and over viaducts like the restored wooden structure at Muttontown Gully. When is a railway not a railway, yet owes its existence and fascination to the fact that it used to be a real railway? When it's a Rail Trail of course. For environmentalists it's a great way to run a railway. No diesel, coal or oil-fired fall-out or pollution (a few horse droppings though). No excessive train noise.

There are spin-offs too for locations near the Rail Trail: St. Bathans, Naseby and MacRaes gold mine; Moonlight, where Ben has made his home in a stone cottage; Land Art Park and Hayes Engineering works at Oturehua.

'You can pretend you are a train as you go through abandoned tunnels and cross bridges and culverts.' Dan, a young American from Arizona, flushed with success and the keen Central Otago air, presents his impression of the Rail Trail as the real train — the TGR service from Middlemarch back through the gorge to Dunedin — inches away from the platform.

'Did you make train noises?' Russ asks.

'I was tempted. A woman waved at me at Omakau and I almost felt compelled to let forth with a whistle blast.'

The return journey, like most, seems to take less time than the outward jaunt. In the case of the train from Middlemarch it's probably true, thanks to the fact that we are now essentially heading downhill.

'What's with those hills of Central?' Dan asks. 'Those fertiliser pilots forgot to do the hills, I reckon.'

He is referring to the distinctly two-toned hues of Central Otago, better represented further in where the old line used to go, and the Rail Trail has taken over. Brown hills sprinkled with schist and tussock stud the green fields, giving the impression that selective top dressing may have left the less accessible hills to fend for themselves.

I am reminded of the first time I travelled on the Central Otago line back in the 1970s. Back then the well-worn Vulcan railcar provided a local stopping service full of locals. Farmers and their wives returned to lonely farming fortresses among the rocky outcrops. School kids treated the Vulcan as a school bus and had to be kept in line by the guard. Nanas knitted between refreshment stops.

'*Do you realise, Ben, that we've been to Middlemarch in the middle of March?*'

'*Good line Theroux, but it's actually the middle of April.*'

Dan is carrying a couple of cameras, a camcorder and a cell phone and Ipod. As we descend through the Taieri Gorge he begins shooting off film at speed. The camcorder is sitting on his shoulder like a contented pet parrot. At times he appears to be shooting from the hip as well with a sophisticated little digital number.

Despite Dan's new technology I am taken back to a magical day in 1971 — the first time I travelled through the Taieri Gorge. We set out early from Alexandra in the days when such an option was still possible. The sheer majesty of the old line in mid-winter, with snow caking the moon rocks and the remarkable two-tone landscape Dan has been talking about, threatened to take the edge off the scenic beauty of the gorge. It had already been a longish day when the rattling, faded red railcar commenced negotiating what we considered to be the last leg of the journey before pulling into Dunedin. A bit of a river gorge up ahead, we figured. We'd come across those before. The North Island had a few.

We had been allocated sensible seats on a regular, scheduled New Zealand Rail service. Unfortunately we were on the 'blind' side of the railcar, which reduced the magic of the first leg of the gorge meander. Back then too, just like the Christchurch to Greymouth railcar, such train journeys were seen as utilitarian, necessary and a tad boring. There was little of today's justifiable glorification of world-class scenery. It may have been a case of familiarity breeding contempt but there was also something in the lack of status afforded New Zealand Rail services in the 60s and 70s that rubbed off on Kiwis. Mediocrity finds its own level. It didn't help that few tourists travelled New Zealand rail back then. Perhaps if there'd been a sprinkling of enthusiastic Americans or Japanese amongst our cautious Kiwi retinue, we might have come to the realisation that in getting from A to B we were traversing versions of scenic paradise. You don't know what you've got until other people — foreign tourists mainly — wax lyrical.

I recalled a stark image from nearly 40 years ago. As I craned my neck to better appreciate the Taieri scenery, my view was partly obscured by a middle-aged man in a suit, sitting bolt upright and staring straight ahead. I wondered if he was blind; otherwise he would surely have been sucked in by the rugged grandeur.

'One man's back yard, another man's paradise.' A line from some unspecified song returned. The tall, suited man probably travelled that route every week, perhaps even on a daily basis. He might have been a pioneer commuter, 1971 vintage. Then again the corsage in his buttonhole could have meant he was on his way to a Dunedin funeral. He might even have been grieving.

The railcar was full and there was no viewing platform.

OPPOSITE As the train edges past schist columns the Taieri River trickles through the gorge.

We were trapped, staring at rock walls or variously attempting to sneak a view around the bolt-upright man with his prominent features and rigid demeanour. Beyond Christmas Creek though, the line crossed the river to the other bank and we had an untrammelled view of the gorge at last.

The success of the TGR is partly due to the altered focus of Kiwi travellers. Forty years ago people travelled this route to attend funerals or to get to and from school or visit the 'big smoke', Dunedin. They had to be somewhere at a prescribed time. In 2007 they are travelling because they can. It's a leisure thing.

In 2007 we wind back through the Notches and Flat Stream. Suddenly, with Dan from Arizona now sharing our enclosure, such reaches take on a different aspect. Dan wants to know if the Notches derived its name from wild shoot-outs among the rocks in the 1880s with dead-eye Dicks notching up conquests with their six-shooters. Or pick-axes. Barewood Creek and Deep Stream are known to us and their wild beauty is reinforced as we travel back across their distinctive formations. Hindon, Ross Point Tunnel and then Christmas Creek are soon upon us.

Christmas Creek. What a name. Nola's notion of a café in the middle of nowhere — the Christmas Creek Café — returns. If nothing else, it's time someone wrote a ballad about the deprivations of the workers who hacked the line through these inhospitable ramparts. At Christmas Creek steel girders were laid on rock pylons hewn out of the very outcrops and rock spurs that studded the route, by construction workers who, back in the late 1870s, relied on pick and shovel and back-breaking labour. I imagine

Nola's great-grandfather teetering on ledges and ekeing out an existence.

Meanwhile the internal life of the TGR train shifts. Joe, one of the train attendants, is now doubling as souvenir salesman. It is almost like happy hour. I am reminded of the orchestrated romps that featured on the Coast Starlight from Seattle to Los Angeles with Jose the barman taking on the role of on-board magician and resident raconteur as the wine-tasting for Californian millionaires and their wives was augmented by 'entertainment factors' in the observation car.

Later, I came across the versatile Jose cleaning the downstairs toilets while passengers nodded off upstairs near Klamath Falls, Oregon.

'You're a busy man, Jose.'

'On this service you have a lot of balls in the air at any given time.'

I am right back there again as Joe announces that wooden whistles like the one he is now peddling were snapped up just the day before by more than 100 American tourists off a cruise ship at Port Chalmers. They paid $15 each. The whistles make the sound of old steam engines when you blow vigorously. Today, Joe is offering them for $10. The Nelsonians buy two, one for each couple. The quieter of the two men spends the next 15 km down past Little Mount Allan, Mount Allan and through the Mount Allan Tunnel blowing hell out of the wooden curiosity. The sound is evocative of the days when AB steam engines echoed up around the Taieri gulches and schist columns.

As well as the whistles, teddy bears are on sale for $19. TGR pens, caps, calendars, key rings, badges and

magnets are a healthy sideline. You can even buy pins and teaspoons as mementoes of your trip and specially commissioned videos, DVDs and print publications provide a pictorial record. Kids, and there are a lot on board, become animated during 'happy hour'. The diversion makes for a jovial interlude.

Towards the end of the journey the train pulls into a loop line at North Taieri, not far from Wingatui Junction. We are here because another TGR service up the Taieri Gorge to Pukerangi requires the single line. We are back on the flat — 34 m above sea level — and everything is, sadly, coming to an end. Russ and I wander out to the viewing platform for a final round of photos. Dan and the Nelsonians follow. There is quite a cluster of us hovering, aware that we are not permitted to leave the train but becoming a little unsettled by the lack of motion. Another train — it could be a track maintenance retinue — occupies the other line. Questions are raised regarding the efficacy of the 2.30 train to Pukerangi edging past on a loop that already shelters a train of sorts.

Off in the distance the main line to Invercargill arcs away towards the deep south. Behind us the sacred Taieri Gorge lies in wait for another trainload of tourists to be transfixed by its unusual and unexpected charms.

Dan from Arizona swigs quietly from a long can of energy drink. 'Topping up the tanks,' he reckons. Nola, windswept, peers anxiously into the murky distance. Russ takes one last shot of the stationary adjacent train, which includes a tamper wagon, utilised, we learned earlier, to ensure the tracks are an adequate distance apart at all times.

Suddenly we are moving again and just beyond the utility train the 2.30 service can be seen waiting patiently on the same siding. I lose count of the number of carriages but they are all full to overflowing. While much of the New Zealand passenger train system grapples with problems of patronage, the TGR has got it right. We wave spontaneously as the faces of perfect strangers flit past.

'I think I saw Winston Peters,' Russ blurts. Winston Peters is a well-known politician. A populist, he tends to pop up in unlikely places. Then again it could be a nuclear physicist from Nantucket.

There is another stop a few kilometres further on, until the all-clear to clatter on to the main line sounds. Then we're racing back through the Dunedin suburbs like a 1950s suburban hop, through the Caversham Tunnel, around the fringes of Carisbrook and down into Dunedin Station.

According to sources that may or may not be authentic, trains used to stop on the rim of the old Carisbrook ground during the course of significant rugby matches. Pictures of test match settings at Dunedin's 'House of Pain' from the 1950s have revealed trains parked up on the rail incline, sharing an excellent vantage point with non-paying rugby fans on the railway embankment as the Springboks from South Africa and Lions from Britain did their best to put the All Blacks away. Signal stop, the old train drivers used to claim. The Limited to Invercargill, or suburban shimmies to Mosgiel, needed to proceed with caution around the perimeter of the park. One train driver, an avowed rugby fan, reckoned he saw three of All Black Don Clarke's world record six penalty goals bisect the posts in 1959 when an under-firing All Black team pipped the

OPPOSITE One of ten tunnels on the stretch from Wingatui to Middlemarch.

British Lions at the post. His train was predictably late on arrival but he was able to attribute that to 'distraction on the track'. I am reminded of the situation in my home town of Te Kuiti, where a branch line skirted Rugby Park. On Saturday afternoons when Colin Meads' Waitete or King Country teams were doing battle, the driver would pull up short of his limeworks destination, abandon his shunt, and slip into Rugby Park to watch the action. The fireman was always close on his heels. Further distractions were cited as reasons for late fulfilment of the shunt's duties.

There are no big games at Carisbrook today and we, if anything, gather speed around the fringes of the scene of some of New Zealand rugby's pivotal moments. Dan likens it to Yankee Stadium or the Sugar Bowl. Nola, coming to the discussion from an oblique angle, suggests she could reinstate the sugar bowl and other 1950s sweet-tooth artefacts at her hypothetical Christmas Creek Café. Beyond the Caversham Tunnel she mentions, almost in passing, that she and her husband own a café in Nelson. Perhaps the Christmas Creek Café will not remain forever hypothetical. I suggest that because of all that schist, variations on the Hard Rock Café theme might be appropriate.

Finally as the late sun shows signs of setting, the Taieri Gorge Limited eases into Dunedin station. It's good to be back, but it would have been even better to remain locked within the walls of the gorge on a train that went up and back indefinitely.

A measure of any given train's fascination is the number of brochures and flyers you unjumble from your travel bag on returning home. Just as I want the Taieri Gorge Limited to carry on indefinitely into the elevated lunar reaches, I pine for a lone brochure among the keepsakes and mementoes that hints at something we missed. A branch, a fork, a siding even that delves further into the wondrous Taieri Gorge hinterland. A lost loop we would come back to and travel on, through a unique landscape where roads, essentially, still don't go. In the end I reconcile myself to having had the privilege of travelling on all that is available, along one of the world's great tourist railways.

Postscript

One vague and minor niggle relating to the TGR trip to Middlemarch was the fact that a steam engine wasn't pulling its weight at the head of the train. It was encouraging to learn from one of the train staff, when I made my feelings known, that steam had indeed returned to the route in April 2001. A Mainline Steam Trust excursion powered by AB663 had become the first train in 30 years to be hauled by the iconic AB locomotive class. Of course there have been practical reasons for the lack of steam power on the line. The absence of water tanks to feed the engines is one. But who knows. The cost of modifications to allow steam engines to operate on a regular basis may not be that prohibitive. One suspects the popularity of the trains through the Taieri Gorge would not be diminished by the introduction of steam haulage.

③ THE PIGROOT CONNECTION: THE SEASIDER

DUNEDIN TO PALMERSTON

The Taieri Gorge Railway runs another train, quite apart from the famous gorge services. Taking advantage of the fact that the Main Line South still hosts freight services, where regular passenger trains also used to run, the TGR has instigated a jaunt that skirts Dunedin harbour and the Otago coast through its most scenic, maritime extremes, before setting down inland at the small town of Palmerston.

A few years back some friends and I were talking about the most likely lines for special tourist trains in New Zealand. There had been some interesting proposals. One of the ideas was a train running from Dunedin to about Palmerston. (Someone suggested Shag Point for reasons that he considered obvious, others Oamaru, the birthplace of writer Janet Frame.) The sea-girt nature of the journey, the history (of which we don't have much in New Zealand), and the spectacular climb above Blueskin Bay were all solid reasons for introducing a specifically appointed tourist train. We even had name proposals for the service. The Gothic Daylight, paying homage to the perceived gothic aspects of Dunedin. The Victorian was another suggestion, based on the Victorian era stone settlement of Oamaru. The Oamaru Oatmeal was a suggestion based on indulgent word play and the fact that oatmeal has long been considered the breakfast of champions for citizens of the Edinburgh of the south, at least by us northerners.

The Whisky Flyer was another. Whisky Chaser was touted as the relief service — the extra train utilised on busy days and Robbie Burns' birthday.

When the Southerner stopped running the nation was plunged into disbelief. The oldest main line in New Zealand, involving vital cities like Christchurch, Dunedin and Invercargill, no longer had a public passenger service. It was a dark moment in the history of rail in New Zealand. But in subsequent years the TGR conjured up the Seasider, exactly the sort of train rail pundits and sensible tourist operators had been talking about for some time, certainly since the Southerner was axed.

Riding on the Seasider is another step back in time. The TGR service travels along that section of the South Island Main Trunk that was opened on 7 September 1878, after the construction gangs working from Christchurch and Dunedin finally met at Goodwood just south of Palmerston. The fact that the line north from Dunedin

had advanced only 57 km when it met the line heading south, 310 km from Christchurch, highlighted the ease of construction across the Canterbury Plains and the difficulty facing railway workers confronted with the hills and bluffs that today mark much of the Seasider's route.

It may be a rule of thumb, when judging the scenic splendour of any given rail journey, that the rate of construction makes a useful gauge of the line's appeal. An easy gambol over flat plains or rolling downs, while pleasant enough for the traveller, and certainly more straightforward for construction teams, cannot compare to finding and building a way through difficult terrain. That's what makes the course of the Seasider spectacular.

The ocean aspect from the outset is alluring, the folds of harbour water shadowed by the muted sun and pastel morning hues of the Otago Peninsula setting the scene for a unique train ride. The climb up around the curve, with the delightful old buildings of Port Chalmers nestling below reminds you that Dunedin is about as venerable as New Zealand gets and alerts you to the fact that the route of the Seasider is about to become challenging.

Port Chalmers is a picturesque town clustered around a modern container port, located 12 km around the harbour. It is dominated by nineteenth century buildings and is in the process of being made over. A thriving artistic cabal has much to do with the growing desirability of Port Chalmers. The main street already has more galleries and craft and antique establishments than real shops and people are starting to visit the town in greater numbers. Beyond the town the historic coastal walk offers sweeping views of the harbour and Otago Peninsula.

Port Chalmers is served by a short branch railway line that leaves the Seasider route on the main south line at Sawyers Bay. It was originally part of the Dunedin and Port Chalmers Railway Company line, built in 1873, linking Dunedin with Port Chalmers. It has the distinction of being the first standard gauge railway in New Zealand. The TGR services pass through a short tunnel to the wharves, where they meet incoming cruise liners.

Before the train disappears into the 1400-m Mihiwaka tunnel, views of Careys Bay and Deborah Bay, seemingly suspended below us, are picture-postcard perfect on this slow, settled, partly-cloudy morning. Out on the viewing platform of the heritage carriage the air tingles. Just the thing to lift the weight of a latish night.

A young English woman who is also taking the keen air is off on the first leg of a 'Railroad to Gold Tour' jaunt. From Palmerston, our eventual destination, she will catch a bus initially to McRaes Gold Mine. From McRaes she will head south-westward to Pukerangi where the matchless Taieri Gorge train completes the circle by returning her to Dunedin at 6.30 pm. We will have completed our return journey long before that, or flagged down a bus heading north.

Suddenly the train enters the Mihiwaka Tunnel and darkness descends. The sounds of the train are multiplied. It's an interesting experience being whisked through the bowels of a large hill with nothing between you and the tunnel walls but deep blackness and circling winds that prompt a clutching at headgear and a gripping of the guard rail with greater intensity. I suspect the train staff might prefer us to be back in the carriage at times like this, but it's an exhilarating experience. One day TGR may even charge extra for this adrenalin rush.

As we emerge into the diffuse light the line continues to climb. Off to the right the Purakanui Inlet glistens in the half-light as the emerging sun edges closer. Beyond the inlet the mouth of Otago Harbour can be seen in the distance. I recall the series of wonderful animated photos of steam locos chuffing uphill, hauling the old Limited passenger train or heavy, long-winded mixed goods towards Dunedin. A place called Mitchie's Crossing springs to mind. Don't know if it still exists, but there's little reason to suspect it doesn't.

The Seasider is riding the crest of a line of hills that affords outstanding views of the Pacific Ocean. Soon, in a dramatic moment, we have penetrated another tunnel before emerging on a ledge high above the entrance to Blueskin Bay. Suddenly the train feels more like a low-flying aircraft winging in over the Otago coast. There doesn't seem to be much territory between the train's course and the gaping, dark blue waters. Tales of the Herculean effort required to scratch a rail right-of-way around these cliffs come to mind. Initially the line fairly clung to a modest cleavage, so much so that Victorian-era passengers blanched at the prospect of taking the train along the precipitous cliffs. Some preferred to travel north by boat. To appease these less intrepid travellers a more generous ledge and extra tunnel were hacked out of the rock face and the speed of trains reduced to 10 mph.

But no calamities ever occurred on this stretch. No express train came to grief and tumbled hundreds of feet into the estuary. Histrionics aside, the steady crawl around the cliffs of Blueskin Bay is like no other on the New Zealand rail network. Within the space of less than half an hour we have gone from the sea-level aspect of the departure along the watery arm of Otago Harbour to the awe-inspiring westward (at one point it is actually due southward) tip-toe above Blueskin Bay. Only a train would bother to bring you out at such a point and in such a casually brilliant manner.

The young Englishwoman suggests that perhaps the

The maritime aspect, as the train climbs beyond Port Chalmers.

construction gangs could have contemplated the expansive notion of a bridge across the entrance to the bay, linking up with the peninsula that, in effect, makes Blueskin Bay the archetypal bay. Perhaps a deep and descending tunnel could have led to the line seeing the light of day at a level where such an ambitious crossing could have been made. The downside of that proposal would have been the loss of the spectacular sea-girt course that has fellow passengers scrambling to our side of the train where all the excellent marine activity is unfolding.

As the line descends towards Waitati a thin beach appears miles below. It is possible to make out a group of temporary beachcombers fossicking and fishing the outlet. Despite the apparent distance you can see them waving as one at the passing train. It's the least we can do to wave back. Perhaps they are a group of doctors from Doctor's Point near the headland. According to the on-board commentary a number of Dunedin doctors in earlier times established a community on the point and commuted to town. Perhaps they caught an old steam-drawn stopping service.

Off in the distance, around the bay, you can see a Toll Rail freight train pulling out of Warrington. The waters of Blueskin Bay are calm and reflective, in more ways than one. In the photo I take from the moving Seasider the freight train will be reflected in the millpond as it scurries off to find a passing loop at Evansdale.

The train descends into Blueskin Bay, named after a prominent local Maori many years ago who sported expansive tattoos, passing through Waitati near sea level. As the Seasider gathers speed, the freight train waits in the loop as we head for the quaint sea-side settlement of Warrington. The latter is laid out on sloping, tiered territory that appears to extend all the way down to the Pacific. From Warrington we are able to look back across the water to see the southbound freight taking on the grade above Blueskin Bay.

Sir Truby King, well known for his pioneering work with newborn infants, was for over 30 years superintendent of the old psychiatric hospital at Seacliff. After the Seasider climbs beyond Warrington and edges along the green hills angling down to the Pacific, vague relics and a few outbuildings of Seacliff Hospital appear in overgrown pockets.

A small white dog chases the train as we pass through a settlement that used to be dominated by the hospital's magnificent stone buildings, designed by R. A. Lawson. His fee was the most generous ever paid in the days when New Zealand was a colony. Magnificent the Oamaru stone buildings may have been, but they were seriously flawed. For a start the foundations on notoriously unstable country were suspect. However, under Truby King's direction Seacliff was transformed from a prison into a hospital and, although it had its critics, it continued in this capacity until 1972, when the last of the patients were transferred to a new facility nearby at Cherry Farm.

An old two-storeyed homestead belonging to Sir Truby King survives at Karitane. It was here that King founded the Plunket Society, the organisation charged with ensuring that newborn babies and their mothers received state-funded support. New Zealand led the world in childcare at the time and Karitane nurses, the minders charged with carrying out Truby King's vision, took their name from the picturesque settlement that is receding now as the train curves inland towards Waikouaiti.

Waikouaiti is a locality of significance. It is the oldest European settlement in Otago. When Dunedin's first settlers arrived, Waikouaiti was Otago's main port, based on the wide sea confluence of the Waikouaiti River as it discharges into Waikouaiti Bay, which dominates the landscape from the train windows. It is a spectacular vista, with the double indentations of the cosy cove and white sands of Karitane's beach and beyond, a spiny peninsula confining the outflow of the Waikouaiti River.

The development of a more direct road to Dunedin led to the decline of Waikouaiti as a place of significance. Despite the fact that Otago's first wool clip was exported from here, the business emphasis rapidly shifted south to Dunedin, or along the new road, away from the seafront settlement.

The Seasider stops just this side of the Waikouaiti River. Off to the west the abandoned buildings of the psychiatric hospital at Cherry Farm poke through the trees. Someone mentions that they think it might be a cheese factory now. It is a lonely setting. The rising noreaster shreds the tussock. Dark, estuarine waters and multi-coloured marine vegetation stud the landscape to the east. The ocean isn't far away. Evidence of its presence may have enlivened the scene. The sky has suddenly turned a drab, mottled grey. Not far up the track a place called Flag Swamp nestles. Beyond that an ambitiously named Pleasant River flows into the sea. Then comes Pleasant Valley, which used to be the site of a sanatorium.

It is now closed of course. The sky continues to lower. Eventually the train begins moving again and the sense of relief at leaving this lonely wasteland is tangible.

Many years ago my wife and I toyed with the idea of moving to this hinterland — she to work as a nurse at Cherry Farm, me to land on my feet in the genuinely pleasant settlement of Warrington with a view to working in Dunedin and a view of the Pacific to die for. Then the era of psychiatric hospital closures began. The plan was abandoned.

But even then it felt like an abandoned place. Once, while I was travelling on the Southerner service, the train stopped at the same spot. The sense of isolation and windswept loneliness was intense. Sometimes it's best if the train passes right on through. The longer you linger along such stretches the more desolate they become.

You can't fault the wavers though. People waving at trains. It's an old-time gesture that lifts the spirits and harks back to the days when New Zealanders in every corner of the country waved at passing trains. It now seems to be a particularly Otago gesture. Near Goodwood, site of the driving of the last spike in the Invercargill to Christchurch main line, a group of workmen gathered around an earthmoving machine, wave at the train. A farmer ploughing a field waves. A brace of baseball-capped youths beyond Goodwood wave. Kids on bikes wave, and an old woman hanging out washing.

Perhaps it's a conditioned reflex. Certainly since the Southerner stopped running, this has been the only regular passenger train through here. Perhaps they are smitten by the same loneliness I feel. Eventually, you are

The author scribbles frantically as dramatic panoramas unfold through the heritage carriage windows.

pleased to wave back. God help us if the people of Otago ever stop waving at the train, I suggest to a middle-aged woman grappling with a malfunctioning camera.

'Seems to be, the further south you go the more the people wave at the trains,' she ventures.

'Must be a lot of waving on the Invercargill to Bluff branch,' I reply.

Finally we arrive at Palmerston, a town of 1300 people. A branch line inland to Dunback (and back) used to render the settlement a railway junction. The station has been made over. It is dark blue where it sits on its arcing platform on the South Island Main Trunk. The bright yellow of the TGR carriages is heightened by the subdued blue Palmerston station. The Seasider comes to rest and we filter into the small town, eager for the gift shops and nationally-ranked mutton pies.

Palmerston is also the junction of State Highway 1, the main arterial link between Christchurch and Dunedin, with the 'Pigroot' (SH85) heading inland to the Maniatoto plains and the old Central Otago goldfields. Palmerston is also handy to beaches visited by seals and yellow-eyed penguins, and Moeraki, a few kilometres north, is the site of the famous spherical boulders that lie clustered on the beach.

In the not-so-old days the prospect of waiting around at Palmerston for the north-bound Southerner would have been an option. Now, in 2007, it's a matter of opting for a bus to Christchurch or, in a moment of inspiration, returning to Dunedin on the Seasider and later taking a plane.

It may have been the mutton pies. Or the continuing friendliness of people from Otago. When the Seasider

pulls out of Palmerston on its way back to Dunedin, we are on it. No one suggested that this rail pilgrimage should be a gallop. Besides, it's a lonely ride bucking across the Canterbury Plains to Christchurch on a bus.

It's funny what you see on return journeys, even a middle-distance one like the Seasider from Palmerston back to Dunedin, compared to the view on the initial journey. The tide is now out and that makes for variant seascapes. The different angle of approach — north to south — throws up landscapes too, that you swear were not there on the morning ride.

Return journeys often seem to take less time. Psychologists and philosophers may have written treatises on the subject, but whether fact or perception, the experience is undeniable. The Seasider leaves Palmerston heading south at 1.00 pm. When we pull into Dunedin it seems like half an hour has been culled from the operational time, although the train is on schedule.

As we pull out of Palmerston a young Kiwi woman who wasn't on the incoming journey (she'd been visiting McRaes gold mine after coming off the Central Otago Rail Trail), shares several theories about time. Apparently by heading south, basically downhill in global terms, there is less gravitational resistance. That would make you travel faster, although it doesn't explain our arrival on time into Dunedin. She also suggests that in the western world we have become time-poor. Perhaps phenomena like return journeys seem to occupy less time because of our mindsets as time-paupers.

By the time we leave Palmerston, the early morning overcast has cleared and the return trip promises to highlight the Otago coastline in an even more sparkling manner. Many passengers, having done with the mutton pies of Palmerston, are on the return journey too. Ed, an elderly American, is a newcomer though he seems a little put out about something.

As the Seasider speeds back through Goodwood he explains his disappointment, disgust really, that he has been unable to catch the now defunct Southerner, which used to link Christchurch, Dunedin and Invercargill. As Russell my travelling companion and I drink a coffee toast with paper cups to the Seasider, Ed says:

'Drinking a toast with paper cups, huh. What's the occasion? One of you guys had twins?'

When we explain that we are celebrating the fact that a train service, even a truncated one, has returned to this hallowed stretch of track, Ed winces.

'They up and axed the goddamn Southerner and you guys get off on this itty-bitty train? I'll bet you guys sat around and let the powers-that-be kill the Southerner. Call yourself good Kiwis.'

The American has been hoping to travel as far as Invercargill on the Southerner. He's done the trip twice before and because he considers New Zealand to be a functional western democracy, he believed the service would still be in place when he needed to use it again. Or at least an equivalent train. We explain about the privatisation of New Zealand Rail, the corporatisation under the Labour Government when market force idealogues were pulling the strings — and the plugs.

'You should have pulled the goddamn stop cord, guys. Now you take a look at Amtrak in my country. Federal agencies stepped in to shore up dwindling passenger services, but they didn't can them. No sir.'

'Hopefully that's the next turn of the railway wheel in New Zealand.' I try to sound convincing but Ed's wince returns. The Seasider returns to the sea beyond the lonely reaches of Waikouaiti, where a prolonged drought is browning the paddocks. This way, heading south, it is possible to get a better perspective on the complex coves of Waikouaiti Bay and the Karitane inlet. The untrammelled early afternoon sun turns the ocean a deeper blue. Not like the opaque pastels of the morning run.

'I didn't think that sort of corporate crap would catch you Kiwis out,' Ed continues. 'A great little country — a goddamn paradise — and you allow yourselves to get corporatised. Sell off the rail as if it's for sale. How the hell am I going to get from Dunedin to Invercargill?'

'Bus.'

'You still got those?'

Ed is understandably taciturn. Not that he is an out-and-out rail fan, but he does appreciate the advantages of rail: the fact that you can move about on a train, get to know the people, grab a bite to eat from the buffet, have a drink, sluice it unmentionably down the toilet. You can't do such things on a bus while you're bouncing around like jumping beans in a bottle. Then he compares our roads to his heart arteries — narrow and awaiting major surgery.

In May 2008 the New Zealand government did in fact buy back the railways. The next turn of the railway wheel had come to pass.

Heading back through Seacliff and Warrington, the wide Pacific gleams.

Returning through the Mihikawa tunnel reminds me of the time a prominent Dunedin rugby coach ran his players through the bore with the threat of an approaching train running them down . . .

'So, how am I going to get to Invercargill?' Ed's question isn't really a question.

'You could fly.'

'What? With these arms?' Ed makes like a Canada goose, wincing even more as he fires up the arthritis that afflicted both shoulders.

This time round we are climbing the gradient above Blueskin Bay as we share a conciliatory beer with Ed. We make it our shout. It seems the least we can do given our collusion in the collapse of the Southerner. From Waitati, up the grade, the ocean vistas all but swallow you. Small Saturday boats bob on the horizon as the Seasider clings even more precariously to the cliff face, like a roller coaster heading for the beginning of the downhill slalom. This incredible engineering feat by the construction gangs back in the 1870s is toasted, this time with aluminium cans.

The afternoon sun glances off the estuarine waters of Purakanui Inlet out to the west. The mood and exchanges in the carriage, now that Ed has ceased winging, is nothing compared to recollections of the grim skirmishes associated with the Purakanui hinterland during the years of the inter-hapu difficulties of Ngai Tahu, the predominant South Island Maori tribe. The site of Mapoutahi pa, the object of the in-fighters' intentions, is located on the coast jutting out into the ocean. Many tales are told of the attempts made to storm the pa, with thwarted warriors variously leaping into the cold sea when threatened or escaping up vine ladders along the cliffs to Doctor's Point.

Out on the viewing platform of the restored 1930s TGR carriage that has seen us incubated in a time capsule for a good part of the day, it is easy to imagine what it must have been like to travel this stretch in the old days. The keen ocean air, the rattle and hum of steel on steel, the pungency of diesel smoke in the tunnels, admittedly less pervasive than the acrid steam engine exhaust, the gaping sea views as the train reveals the homeward-bound views of the far-off heads of the Otago Harbour.

Returning through the Mihikawa tunnel reminds me of the time a prominent Dunedin rugby coach ran his players through the bore with the threat of an approaching train running them down, in a typically Antipodean attempt to overhaul the speed of his squad. Rugby was for keeps back then. Otago, the province, held the Ranfurly Shield, symbol of provincial New Zealand rugby supremacy, and the coach was intent on retaining the trophy.

Beyond the tunnel (there don't appear to be any skeletons of 1940s rugby players cluttering up its recesses) the Seasider angles down towards the Otago Harbour, past Port Chalmers and Sawyers Bay and on to the homeward, sea-level approaches. A strange, unscheduled mist has descended, muffling the horizon. This is typical of Dunedin, apparently. After all, it's not that far from Antarctica and sudden dismal weather changes are to be expected.

Yet the swirling fog does not induce melancholy, as we have been told it can. It has been a good day on one of the great New Zealand train rides, rendered twice as memorable by our impromptu decision to treat it as a round trip. Mind you, one or two haunting issues have invaded my thoughts.

As the train descended through Port Chalmers, I cast a backward glance towards the settlement of Aramoana at the harbour entrance. In 1990 a lone gunman went on a killing spree, accounting for 13 souls, before he himself died. Across the harbour at Anderson's Bay four years later, someone killed five members of the Bain family and the old home in Every Street was later razed by fire. Back up the track the sad institutions, now closed, at Seacliff and Cherry Farm, have added to the sombre mix. Every Street could be any street in New Zealand. Aramoana is the kind of rustic Kiwi beach settlement where nothing ever happens.

They reckon one of the sadder services along this stretch in earlier times was the Sunday train that took the 'loonies' back to Seacliff Hospital from points north like Ashburton, Timaru and Oamaru. Janet Frame, the New Zealand writer who spent time in Seacliff, described the service in such a bone-scraping way that she got to the very core of the situation: the devastated families, the anxious patients, the antipathy of 'normal' passengers, the gothic horror of the forbidding hospital buildings, the irony of the gorgeous sweeping sea views.

I looked around the carriage at the 'ordinary people'. Did they know where I had been? If they knew, would they look at me and then turn away quickly to hide the fear and fascinated curiosity as if they were tasting an experience which — thank God, they thought — they would never know but about which they wondered furiously, fearfully? If they knew about me, would they try to find a sign, as I had done when I, too, used to stare at the 'loonies' on Seacliff Station.

Even the ocean aspect of Seacliff was unsettling. This was no cosy, welcoming cove, just a massive vertiginous cliff plunging down to the remote, seemingly horizonless Pacific. An agoraphobic's nightmare. A displaced person's trigger to seek out familiar islands and friendly lights in welcoming homes. The sense of melancholy was tangible.

And yet as the Seasider gallops through Ravensbourne, with its wharf extending out into the harbour, a group of bystanders waves enthusiastically at the train. Ed, his mood lifting like the mist, has decided to catch a bus to Invercargill; after taking a look at the Taieri Gorge Railway to Pukerangi that will surely rekindle his faith in New Zealand trains. A sense of joviality now prevails.

The Otago Harbour is still a picturesque sight even though the tide is out now and boats are aground in the small bays. Clusters of locals peck around in the exposed sand and mud for shellfish, taking their time to wave muddied hands at the train.

'It's a nice harbour,' a Dutch fellow-passenger declares. 'We went on a harbour cruise yesterday to look at the harbour. But the boat driver was so young he thought we wanted excitement. So he made his boat go like a racing car, swerving around like a fool. We just wanted to see the sights. My daughters thought it was good but my wife was made almost sick.'

George Troup's magnificent Dunedin Station, as it swallows the incoming Seasider, reminds us that all is not lost. Perhaps it was always meant to be that one day someone would install an Otago coastline round-trip like the Seasider.

After all, the old expresses and limiteds and railcars used to pass through such sacred stretches in the middle of the long haul from Christchurch or Invercargill, at a time when passengers were busy knitting, nodding off or otherwise preoccupied. The sea-girt miles between Dunedin and Palmerston were just another link in the chain of the extended passage along the east coast of the South Island.

As the Seasider slinks to a halt you get to thinking about other distinctive stretches of track on the New Zealand system that may have been taken for granted because they occur during the course of long, exhausting and sometimes distracting journeys. Perhaps these segmented, shorter stretches would lend themselves to additional trains like the Seasider?

We bid farewell to Ed as he goes looking for a bed for the night. Another older gent, a Kiwi, wishes us well.

'Well, at least they still wave at the trains down here,' I yell in affirmation above the skirl and clamour.

'That's because there are so few trains. You'd wave at them too.'

He is at least partly right. It is easy to rhapsodise about the Taieri Gorge Railway and how it has filled a gaping void in New Zealand rail services. While beaurocrats and maverick business operators have variously fumbled and bled much of our passenger train resource dry, the Otago tourist train operators have hit the nail on the head. It helps of course that the TGR can load passengers like cattle directly from cruise liners with names like *Crystal Harmony*. (The love boats, the locals call them, just as they refer to the all-girls' singles train that still vibrates up the gorge to Middlemarch as the 'love train'.)

The city of Dunedin in turn has a love affair with the TGR. My experience on the two routes currently run by the tourist train operation has presented me with matchless scenery, interesting travelling companions and a rekindling of my passion for outstanding railway journeys.

So we fly from Dunedin Airport to Christchurch, winging over a railway line that looks abandoned and lonely. A single freight train courses around Caroline Bay just out of Timaru, but from the plane the rail route across the plains looks bereft.

④ THE FINE LINE: THE TRANZALPINE

CHRISTCHURCH TO GREYMOUTH

I have heard it said that the TranzAlpine train from Christchurch to Greymouth is one of the six best train journeys in the world. I've also heard it said that the four-hour journey through the Southern Alps is one of the seven best rail journeys this side of the Rio Grande.

A TranzAlpine driver signs a tourist's autograph book at Arthur's Pass.

PREVIOUS PAGE The TranzAlpine in characteristic pose. Mountains are never too far away.

And so it goes. I've seen Asian students sleep the journey away, wedged like hung-out-to-dry gropers between their seats and the carriage wall, their mouths opening and shutting involuntarily as if seeking food in their comatose bliss.

You get the feeling that a lot of Kiwis have been slow on the uptake too. Until tourists gave the TranzAlpine a hearty thumbs-up we tended to underrate the service. It had never traversed the main South Island line, you see. The Midland line through the mountains was only a branch line although it had a significant reach. Ross, beyond Hokitika, was the railhead to the south once the Midland line hit the West Coast; Seddonville was the end of the line to the north. Specialised coal trains from Ngakawau, just south of Seddonville, have given the northern fork a reprise in recent years, otherwise it would surely have wizened like so many unfashionable, revenue-losing services off the beaten track.

The Christchurch-Greymouth run developed cult status with me back in the late 1960s. At that time my interest in trains had been rekindled, as much by a Bob Dylan song, 'It takes a lot to laugh, it takes a train to cry', as a serious welling of down-country wanderlust. Earlier, in the 1950s, I recall a black and white glossy photo section in the *Auckland Weekly News* featuring express trains drawn by JA and KB engines with a whole lot of mountains and unfamiliar territory in the background; low-lying lakes reflecting snow-covered domes and the plumes of white steam engine smoke; massive plateaux with no roads or towns or people, just the steel-carriaged expresses; the Grey River brimming with flood waters beside which the steam monsters made the Morris eights and Austin sevens on the adjacent road seem inconsequential.

Not long after the release of the Beatles' 'Sergeant Pepper' album, my mate Russ and I decided to undertake a rail pilgrimage through the South Island. The Auckland to Wellington express took us through the night and after a storm-tossed crossing of Cook Strait we were on our own. The railcar journey from Picton to Christchurch was mindblowing, although Russ had to contend with a corked thigh muscle, an old rugby injury aggravated while trying to get to the bar on the inter-island ferry.

The discovery of gold on the West Coast in the 1860s led to the pushing through of a stagecoach route via Arthur's Pass. Eventually the rail followed although it took the blasting of a long hole — the Otira Tunnel — to see the east side link with the west. This happened in 1923.

By the time we set out from Christchurch Station in 1967, a railcar service had been running for several years. No point pining for a KB or JA-hauled express. You have to move on. But there was a pang of disappointment somewhere within the thrill of broaching the now mythical Midland line. 'Can't buy a thrill,' Dylan sang in 'It takes a lot to laugh, it takes a train to cry', but we had managed, or so we thought. Ten of the new decimal dollars per head.

The railcar reached Springfield in the lee of the mountains, where officials advised us that a slip near Otira Tunnel had condemned us to a long, dispiriting bus ride over the Lewis Pass to the West Coast. We should have de-trained at Springfield and come back later when the slip had been cleared. The train journey was the whole point of the exercise. The bus trip stank. A suitcase toppled out of the rack at Reefton and glanced my head. We had to change vehicles at some wet hole because our bus didn't have the balls to make it. And I left behind a recently purchased copy of 'Bee-Gees First', an album that is still probably in the possession of some deranged drainlayer from Frog Flat Junction.

So, if anybody jibs at taking the TranzAlpine through the mountains, if Asian students see fit not to see a bloody thing, I tend to get testy. As it happened Russ and I came back several years later and got all the way through by railcar. No Otira slip or arthritic Road Services bus was about to stop us. And it was magnificent.

Now in 2007 we are back for more. The TranzAlpine has become a New Zealand success story. It won a tourist award in 1988 and regularly fills a ten-car consist, compared to the pathetic two-car configurations it succeeded in the 1980s.

Until 1993 trains left from Moorhouse Station, a great brick slab of a building that used to dispatch Christchurch suburban trains to Rangiora in the north and offshoots to the Southbridge and Little River branches to the south. For many years there were suburban trains down the Southern Main Trunk and through the Lyttelton Tunnel. The latter linked with the Wellington to Lyttelton overnight ferry. In general Christchurch was a bustling, snorting, steam-hauled field of suburban train operations.

As economic reality bit the Christchurch services receded and the focus shifted to long-distance passenger trains. In 1993, the year that saw the opening of the new Addington Railway Station, laid out where the old railway workshops used to be, the connecting link between North and South, the new umbilicus also came into being. Was it a rebirth?

The TranzAlpine seems very much a well-adjusted child of the modern New Zealand rail system. This is no fledgling service striking out on wooden rails, but rather a high-achieving scion of the family of twenty-first century scenic, long-distance tourist trains.

The wide windows beckon. The plush seats — airline-like — encourage a reflective mood from the outset. If your brief is to take in a power of scenery, you are ideally situated to do so. This line has a past too. Beyond the largely industrial suburb of Sockburn, where the Air Force Museum is located, along with a unique pioneering jetboat factory, a short spur line used to arc south to Addington Raceway, venue for the annual New Zealand Trotting Cup. In the days when locals jumped on a train rather than clambered into cars, such a spur was typical. It closed in 1954.

Hornby, Islington and Templeton rattle past as the TranzAlpine gathers pace. Hornby used to be the junction for the Southbridge Branch and even today still serves industrial connections and sidings. Islington used to boast a freezing works, Templeton a mental hospital.

Two American travellers share our table. They detect a connection between the closure of freezing works and mental hospitals, as we all sip our first coffee. My travelling companion and I don't bother completing the connection. We are focused on the line ahead.

Rolleston, the junction, is upon us. Some years back there was a plan to make Rolleston, named after William Rolleston, Superintendent of Canterbury Province in the mid 1800s, a satellite city of Christchurch. For various reasons the plan was axed and one of the southern suburb's remaining claims to fame is the junction point where the Midland Line, to Greymouth on the West Coast, strikes out. In so doing it enables the TranzAlpine to fulfil its status as the only train in New Zealand to travel from coast to coast — east to west.

We are still on the edge of the Canterbury Plains but once the train has graunched through the junction points, the mountains waiting to be confronted off to the west

become apparent. Aylesbury, Kirwee and Darfield are accounted for as the train barrels towards the Southern Alps. Darfield, 45 km from Christchurch, is the old junction of the White Cliffs branch, a former coal railway that closed in 1962. Nearby Racecourse Hill was the scene of a battle of wits between an extrovert train driver and a highly-strung local school teacher. The train driver had been inclined to blow his engine whistle rather too willingly as his train thundered past the local school. The school teacher allowed the decibels to get to him and took to greasing the section of Midland Line that skirted his school. After several stallings as the driver found he was unable to gain traction, the errant whistling died away.

The TranzAlpine engine whistle blasts occasionally across this stretch where the plains rise to meet the foothills. Sheffield, nearly 60 km from Christchurch and the centre of a prosperous farming district, passes. Sheffield is the old junction of the rural branch line that used to link Oxford with Rangiora, on the Main North Line.

Arriving at Springfield, in the lee of the towering Torlesse Ranges, is a pivotal phase. Behind, the plains shelve back down to Christchurch and the east coast. Before us the promise of passage through the South Island's backbone is assured. Springfield has always been a major stop on the Midland Line: the place where steam engines were changed in the old days, a place worth pausing for simply because from here on in, the Midland Line and the TranzAlpine's passage follow a remarkably different trajectory and scenic route compared to the highway.

Springfield was originally known as Kowhai Pass, a significant journey west that, in stagecoach days, saw

passengers accommodated in the settlement on their way to the mountains. The early tendrils of the Midland Line extended from Rolleston to Springfield by 1880, although the link through the mountains and the West Coast river valleys was not completed until 1923, the year the Otira Tunnel was opened.

In 2007, there is time to wander around the Springfield station precincts after nearly 70 km of travel. The silence is profound. The mountains and foothills loom, sprinkled with snow. Behind and beyond, the receding plains give nothing away. In the distance a lone four-wheel-drive murmurs on a dirt road. Our train is waiting on the SUV's driver, not that we are being delayed by his late arrival. A certain amount of time has been set aside at this station that was rebuilt in 1965 after fire damaged the original building. Hawks hover in the air as passengers inspect the station's visitor centre with its collection of railway memorabilia and in-house café. Up until 1987 Springfield station, a designated Rail Heritage Trust building because of its distinctly 1960s architecture, functioned as a refreshment stop and a quick coffee and muffin (it used to be tea and rock cake) honour its refreshment past.

'Head for the hills,' the diesel engines seem to say as the TranzAlpine throbs away from Springfield Station. There's no turning back as the line curves away from State Highway 73, the Arthur's Pass road, which has shadowed the line all the way from Aylesbury. The remote charm of the TranzAlpine's course is suddenly revealed as the line heads initially due north and then north-east, almost like an airliner seeking to return to its take-off point because of engine gremlins. One of the myths of New

Zealand rail travel is debunked, the one that suggests that railway lines essentially follow the course of major roads. Beyond Springfield and until the Midland Line emerges many miles later, beyond Cass, the TranzAlpine winds through river gorges, past remote lakes, beneath brooding mountains and across braided reaches that can often only be accessed by train.

The mountain scenery is instantly magnetic. Our American friends, with digital camera and cam-corder, repair to the observation car as the mountains close in.

In viaduct country the TranzAlpine negotiates Patterson's Creek viaduct.

OPPOSITE The TranzAlpine in reflective mood at Springfield.

The train climbs, the Americans and others whir and snap. The Kowhai River is crossed, initially on the Big Kowhai Bridge, the line's first viaduct (the original bridge was washed away by flood waters), then the Little Kowhai Bridge hoves into view as the line arches back towards the east. The Waimakariri River Gorge is upon us.

Across the wide braided Waimakariri River several ski chalets and huts stud the river line. What a place to lose yourself. Not so good if you got lost, which is different. Getting away from it all takes on a new perspective up here, little more than a couple of hours from Christchurch.

As we pass through the Kowhai Bush area, foothills begin rising off to the west. Yellow, scrubby expanses flank the tracks, yet the last of the Canterbury paddocks are still green enough and dotted with sheep. Soon Patterson's Creek viaduct is carrying the line west. The contrast with the plains is total. The onset of the mountain scenery has been rapid, like the flicking of a TV remote switch. Sixteen tunnels and five viaducts take the train into a mystical no-man's land. Somewhere near the middle of the TranzAlpine's consist, an old guard's van converted into an open-air viewing vehicle offers time out and time outside. It's a photographer's dream. The Americans excuse themselves again as the scenery becomes dramatic. One of them is a bit hard of hearing. I tell him about the 16 tunnels and he is agreeably surprised that I am a fan of Tennessee Ernie Ford — the American singer whose signature tune was 'Sixteen Tons'. The American sways down the aisle humming the tune. Eventually we follow as the Waimakariri flows beneath us, heading down its 150-km course from the Southern Alps to Pegasus Bay near Kaiapoi, north of Christchurch.

The Torlesse Range angles away to the west, the Puketeraki Range covers the north-east. The Midland line is very much on its own through here. No roads of any description for company through the craggy wilderness.

Staircase on the outer rim of the Torlesse Range is a stunning location. The line has been laid down across a massive rock shelf between the mountains and the river gorge. There used to be a rail settlement up here but nothing remains. Obviously the Staircase viaduct and tunnel have survived, but the sheer magnitude of the landscape and the notion that workmen took it upon themselves to hack the line through this forbidding territory, are thought-provoking. And the train is still only 80-odd kilometres from Christchurch.

The Americans are nonplussed by the physical grandeur of Staircase, surely one of the most spectacular settings on the New Zealand rail system. They emphasise the fact that it has taken the TranzAlpine little more than an hour to get from the plains to the elevated, wild reaches of the Waimakariri Gorge.

Soon the line curves away from the Waimakariri River and enters the Broken River Gorge. The tunnels have been coming thick and fast. Tunnel number ten, at 610 metres in length, is the second longest on the line, exceeded only by the seemingly endless Otira bore further up the track.

The wind is getting up out on the viewing platform and it's sobering to recall that a portion of the Patterson's Creek viaduct was blown askew in a north-westerly gale some years back. We return, a little blue about the gills, to the warmth of the carriage. The train crosses the Broken River Viaduct, an intricate piece of engineering, and the

Sloven's Creek Viaduct which serves to carry the line out of the Broken River Gorge into Sloven's Valley.

We are now well into the journey. As the train continues climbing, Avoca, Craigieburn and Cass slip past. Hard to say if any are settlements as such, although you can imagine unshaven, wild-eyed recipients of Creative New Zealand grants hunkered down in vague collectives, waiting on their muse.

A road of sorts accompanies the line from Avoca, which used to boast a coal mine. Further on at Craigieburn (named after a local sheep station), the line begins descending to the Waimakariri River. Lake Grasmere and Lake Sarah are bisected. Cass was an overnight stagecoach halt built in the old days and in this day and age represents the point where the Midland line reacquaints itself with State Highway 73, last seen at Springfield. Cass used to be a frontier town. Wild cattle shooting was a popular pastime. A more subdued contemporary environment sees botany students from Canterbury University basing themselves in the hinterland and scouring the surrounds for sub-alpine samples.

The highway and railway veer westward beyond Cass into the upper reaches of the Waimakariri River Valley before heading north beside the Bealey River, a tributary of the Waimakariri. The mountains close in further as Arthur's Pass approaches.

In summer, Arthur's Pass is a sanctuary. Cool and collected, it brings a tingle of mystery. You can imagine the late George Harrison of the Beatles stopping off here, as much to tune his sitar as to bland-out in the pristine, upheaved landscape, not far from the meeting point of two tectonic plates, moving at around 2.5 centimetres a year. George, with his single-mindedness, might have hastened the rate of uplift, making for higher mountains — the better to get nearer his maker.

Arthur's Pass is a true alpine railway setting. We could be in Austria or Switzerland. Until 1997 the 14-km electrified stretch of rail that carried trains beyond Arthur's Pass and through the Otira tunnel had the distinction of being the first electrified route in the South Island. In steam days the tunnel presented too many smoke problems and electric engines were deployed to pull trains through the long hole in the Southern Alps.

Even now, with diesel traction providing an uninterrupted motive force, Arthur's Pass, despite the withdrawal of Swiss-style electrics, still resembles a European alpine crossing point. Arthur's Pass station, built in the alpine style after the loss by fire of the original structure in 1966, is one of the most evocative in the New

LEFT Arthur's Pass in winter, the highest station on the line.

OPPOSITE Crossing the Waimakariri River in clearing weather.

Four seasons in one day. The train, about to encounter squally weather, crosses the Taramakau River.

historic walk around Arthur's Pass Village and extending to more demanding forays like the Devil's Punchbowl Falls Walk and the Bridal Veil Walk.

For those staying with the train a gentle walk along the platform presents images of steepling, snow-crowned mountains and lazy coal smoke rising from local chimneys. You may also have an encounter with the cheeky kea birds looking for edible handouts from TranzAlpine passengers before progressing to wanton pecking of rubber seals on parked cars and similar material on carriage exteriors.

Beyond Arthur's Pass the line crosses the Bealey River Bridge, which at 742 metres is not only the highest point on the Midland line but the loftiest point traversed by rail in the South Island. Then comes the Otira Tunnel.

The Otira Tunnel used to be the longest in New Zealand. At 8.5 km it isn't far short of the Rimutaka or Kaimai bores in the North Island. It has the distinction of traversing the upthrust rift of the South Island. That's why it is forced to plummet at a 1 in 33 gradient down into the darkness. The partial plunge takes the breath away as the TranzAlpine gathers speed in the pitch black.

Passing through the Otira Tunnel is like leaving one country and re-emerging in another. It's still New Zealand, but the western side of the Southern Alps — Westland — is so different in terms of vegetation and geography it is easy to imagine that the depths of the Otira Tunnel have generated some sort of time warp. Shaped by heavy rainfall, Westland landscapes contrast sharply with the dry alpine reaches of Arthur's Pass and points further east. Indeed it is coming on to rain as the TranzAlpine follows the course of the Otira River.

Zealand rail system. At 737 metres above sea level it is the highest station in the South Island.

Much coming and going occurs when the TranzAlpine pulls in. Although the Arthur's Pass settlement has only about 50 permanent residents, it provides access to the Arthur's Pass National Park, the fourth largest in New Zealand. Walking tracks radiate out, beginning with the

The Otira Tunnel was the longest in the British Empire and the Southern Hemisphere when it was opened in 1923. In the same year it was deemed to be the seventh longest in the world. These days diesel engines are able to negotiate the bore because of exhaust fume suction ventilation systems.

During the ghostly downhill plunge through the tunnel we strike up an odd conversation with two West Coasters, heading home.

'Have you been to the Wildfoods Festival at Hokitika?' They seem happy to develop the West Coast theme.

'You're talking ferret's lung, bull's semen, cockroach turnovers . . . ?'

'Deep fried goat's throat.'

A gurgle of laughter breaks the ice.

The rainforest advances on the landscape as lakes begin to stud the 'other side'. I once had a dream about this stretch. A Technicolor dream in the depths of a coal-blackened, steam-driven Te Kuiti night. I recalled the spectacular rainforest greens and sky-blue lake reflections as the train I was riding swayed through this version of New Zealand backwater, the bright red carriages drawn by a silent motive force far removed from the grunting, grubby steam engines of the North Island's main trunk. It was a prescient, recurring, dream.

Goat Creek Bridge, Kelly's Creek and Deception River fly past as the TranzAlpine begins its descent to the West Coast lowlands. The settlement of Aickens, named after William Aicken who set up the renowned Aickens Accommodation house, complete with Post Office facilities, features before the line arcs back westward to follow the Taramakau River, associated with greenstone and gold in the 1860s. A gold dredge plied the river here until the early 1980s.

The West Coast rain is falling now as we head west through Jacksons, which, not surprisingly, suffered the loss of its hotel in an 1871 flash flood. The wet charms of the West Coast, with its verdant rainforests and pulsing rivers, are heightened by the sudden deluge.

At Inchbonnie, a name that triggers sniggering from the two young West Coast women sitting opposite us, the line screws back to the north, past Lake Poerua and the equally hilarious Crooked River, Te Kinga, and Ruru, where one of New Zealand's last-gasp steam-operated bush tramways worked the rainforest until 1962. Ruru, Maori for native owl, boasts a station preserved by the Rail Heritage Trust as a fine example of a dogbox structure. An apt place for dogs to catch the TranzAlpine? Or a poignant memorial to Rosie, the border collie who used to meet the TranzAlpine further back along the track on a daily basis, and who accounted for thousands of meat pies presented by train staff?

After a right-angled turn due west, the TranzAlpine comes to rest at Moana, on incandescent Lake Brunner. A more tranquil setting on the New Zealand rail network is hard to imagine. Outsiders are beginning to cash in on its beauty too. Ninety people live in the idyllic lakeside settlement. Christchurch yuppies are said to have targeted the setting and are developing weekend retreats to take advantage of the outstanding fishing, swimming and boating potential. Even the Moana station has unique charms, glorying in the preservation status granted by the Railway Heritage Trust as a classic example of an Edwardian-style rural station.

Moana station sees us wandering along the platform. I'm not sure if we are allowed to. We've followed the smokers, who are puffing earnestly, the thin blue exhaust rising in the crisp air. On the lake, the largest in Westland, the angling sun flickers. The green of the surrounding foothills seems to change hue. I can't remember a more dramatic railway moment, although if we were to arrive by car or walk in from a bush track the scene might be similarly uplifting. But then you think about the rail component. As a rail fan I find any aspect of New Zealand scenery is enhanced when I discover it by train. Railway access is almost a fourth dimension.

A brief sunshower pings off the carriage windows as we move, reluctantly, beyond Moana. The lake waters continue to glisten, a rainbow forming in the lee of the enclosing Hohonu Range.

The Arnold River, which flows out of Lake Brunner, follows the line as far as Stillwater on the Grey. The Arnold is named after Dr Thomas Arnold, headmaster of Rugby School in England between 1828 and 1841; we feel obliged to explain to a Swiss tourist the importance of Rugby School and consequently, the game of rugby to many New Zealanders. The Swiss guy, who looked quite at home earlier as the TranzAlpine negotiated the mountain pass between Arthur's Pass and Otira, mumbles something in mystified French before returning to his red wine.

At Kaimata, almost halfway along the Arnold River, the West Coast girls point out the small hydro-electric station — in fact the smallest with input to the state power grid, a generator of little more than 3600 kw — at which juncture the Swiss chap comes up with a leering comment on the theme of 'size isn't everything'. More giggles and sniggering.

At Kokiri, a few kilometres onwards, a beef slaughterhouse is also highlighted. Most kills are of the Islamic halal variety with beasts being obliged to face Mecca when topped. The grisly result is exported to the Middle East. Once again it is the West Coast girls of wild food fame who bring us up to date with the facts. We are relieved not to receive the information from an onboard al-Qaeda operative.

As we arrive at Stillwater, where the water is anything but still — the Arnold River plummets into the surging Grey for a start — memories wash over me. Back in the late 1960s Stillwater was a decided junction. Not only did the Arnold meet the Grey, but the Buller railway line met the Midland, where you could still catch a railcar to Westport (like a fool I didn't) along the track that today carries coal trains from the mines at Ngakawau, north of Westport, to the Midland line and all the way to Lyttelton Harbour. Stillwater was also an old-style refreshment stop. I remember a particularly molten mince pie, prior to settling back for the rumble down the south bank of the Grey River to Greymouth. After the Stillwater pie I suffered from a temporary grey mouth, which made the final approach even more appropriate.

The Grey River buckets for 121 kilometres from mountain source to the Tasman Sea. Gold and coal have dominated its history. The TranzAlpine gathers speed along its banks as it heads for the coast. Brunner passes,

OPPOSITE 'Like leaving one country and re-emerging in another'. The TranzAlpine encounters the West Coast.

as train staff fuss about in their attempts to have the train in pristine shape when it pulls into Greymouth. Brunner, a significant section of which lies over the river via a suspension bridge, was the site of New Zealand's worst industrial accident in 1896.

Dobson rushes past. The riverside hamlet was named after George Dobson, brother of Arthur Dudley Dobson of Arthur's Pass fame. George Dobson was a surveyor killed by the infamous Burgess gang who figured George was carrying significant amounts of gold. He wasn't.

Finally we pass the settlement of Kaiata, and the train slows as the line reveals homes that, since the major flood of 1998, have perched on stilts above the flood-prone Omotumotu Creek. The Swiss chap and the West Coast girls hover around our enclosure to say goodbye.

The early afternoon sun, peeping through nervous, flitting clouds, glances off the approaching Tasman Sea. The company of perfect strangers on their way home reminds us that trains have a habit of cajoling and calming. The TranzAlpine, because it hightails through some of the most stunning scenery in the world, speeds up the process. We've only been on the train for four hours.

One of the West Coast girls reveals that she used to be a high-flying executive in Wellington. Not quite a CEO, but close enough to feel real affinity with decision making on $100,000 a year. Then something snapped. Redundancy became an option and she took it. They couldn't see her for dust. Computers crashed as she turned her back on privilege that had always struck her as being the female equivalent of the Peter Principle — individuals promoted beyond their ability. The Penelope Principle, someone reckons, although I figure he's making that up.

As the TranzAlpine angles towards Greymouth Station, thoughts again wash over me, even as the Grey River — confined and controlled behind the 'Great Wall of Greymouth' flood bank — washes into the sea. If stressed-out executives, with their multi-tasked meltdowns and post-takeover blues, could be here now on this train, half the counsellors in the brave new world would be out of a job. Mind you, that would create stresses on a brave new front — counsellors needing counsellors. Then again, all they would need to do, between jobs, is get a ticket to ride on the TranzAlpine.

Despite such musings, the facts and figures remain. Greymouth, at the end of the TranzAlpine's route is 231.2 kilometres from Christchurch. It is the largest West Coast town, with a population of 12,900. Thirty fishing boats operate out of the town. Beyond such tangibles, Greymouth is more about a colourful history and a unique ambience — and the Rewanui Incline.

We decide to stay overnight in Greymouth. After four hours of wondrous train travel from Christchurch — through two distinct micro-climates, under the mountainous South Island backbone, up Canterbury fringe river valleys and down the fully-fledged equivalents on the Westland side — it is time to kick back and contemplate. A couple of old friends live at Kumara Junction, south of Greymouth, and my first trip to the West Coast in 10 years seems a good opportunity to catch up — and contemplate.

In the hours between the TranzAlpine's arrival in the early afternoon and the time we are scheduled to be uplifted by our Kumara friends, we hire a car and travel as far as we can up the road that follows the Rewanui Incline's old right of passage. It doesn't go all the way these days, but the climb is enough to bring back the memories of a unique and unforgettable rail experience in a hinterland that has now been sealed off to train fans.

See your own country first. The old mantra extolling the virtues of New Zealand and encouraging Kiwi travellers to check out the backblocks and unbeaten tracks before flying out to Bondi, LA or London, seems to apply specifically to the West Coast of the South Island.

Arriving in Greymouth in a torrential downpour by Fiat railcar in 1971, after swaying down the Grey Valley (beside a Grey River lapping its stopbanks) before pulling into a town that looked like New Zealand in the 1950s, was as good as travelling to a different country anyway. Our hotel was old and angular and creaked as we climbed the stairs. Condensation, the result of Greymouth's bounteous rainfall, mottled flower-patterned wallpaper. Down in the bar a clutch of locals regarded incoming strangers with haunted eyes. Later we learned that most of the drinkers were coalminers, their eyes attributable to coaldust rings where the bath-house soap didn't go.

See your own country first. When in Rome. We took up station at the horseshoe-shaped bar alongside the locals and joined the seven-ounce sweep that saw the barman topping up glasses in an anti-clockwise direction, wiping away residue as the glasses were somewhere between bar top and mouth, before preparing his beer bowzer for another anti-clockwise sweep.

Outside, through the rain, a steam-engine whistle blared. That was the miners' train from Rewanui shuffling into the station. Soon a phalanx of drenched miners off the train were forming a second tier of imbibers aligning themselves around the bar.

We learned about the Rewanui train and the Rewanui Incline. We could have flown out to Wales and experienced similar locales, where miners celebrated another day of survival after a long subterranean shift.

Typically, despite our fondness for rail travel, we had been unaware of the Rewanui Incline. The Rimutaka Incline was mythologised. Everyone, including those for whom rail travel had little attraction, had heard of the world-famous, middle-rail adhesion, Fell-hauled steam trains that thundered up the side of the Rimutaka Ranges carrying people and goods from the Wairarapa to Wellington. Now as we joined the hard-drinking coal miners of Greymouth, in a public bar that soon had surface water lapping around the hastily assembled sandbags at the door, it was possible to imagine that we were in another land. The Republic of the West Coast, a watery outpost that was like no other part of New Zealand we had encountered.

The West Coasters told us about the Rewanui Incline railway and the service we should experience, as champions of rail and upholders of the see New Zealand first philosophy. On any given day, the first service at 6.35 am was the miners train that carried coal workers out over the invariably brimming Grey River and up into the hills to the north of Greymouth. An hour later the return service down the incline provided a commuter service, essentially for women who worked in Greymouth. This

. . . the return service provided a commuter service, essentially for women who worked in Greymouth . . . known as the fanny train in days when political correctness had not bled the language of colour.

service was known as the fanny train in days when political correctness had not bled the language of colour. There was also an early afternoon train known as the wet-timer, catering for miners who worked a shorter shift in damp and dangerous recesses of the mines.

Despite assurances to the contrary, we missed the early train. In July, when we travelled to the 'wet coast', such a service departed and arrived in darkness. We convinced ourselves as we slept through alarms that, in our quest to see New Zealand first we would be better served being able to actually see a slice of New Zealand we hadn't even realised was there.

The wet-timer it was. A Ww tank engine and three wooden carriages waited at the station. With a snort and a blast the engine hauled us out over the Grey River on the S-shaped bridge that vibrated with the buffeting of flood-borne branches and foliage. No one said a word. After all these were coalminers off to do dirty, dangerous

work below ground. There was no Disneyland at the end of the line. In 1967, a year or two before we 'discovered' the West Coast, Greymouth and the Rewanui Incline, 19 miners had lost their lives in the Strongman Mine disaster. Similar mines were about to be worked by many of the men travelling in our carriage.

Having survived the Grey River crossing, the wet-timer gathered what speed it could as it headed north towards Runanga, where a short spur line to Rapahoe, another coal-mining hub, continued due north. The Rapahoe line is still working in 2007 (but it's a shame the Rewanui train no longer runs). The Rewanui line curved north-east through the hills, past Dunollie, and on to the 1 in 26 gradient into the clouds. The rain continued to bucket down as the engine fought the grade along the 5.4 km of track between Dunollie and Rewanui. It was interesting to learn how vital this rail link was in terms of mine access. Rewanui had no road access, although a bike track beside the line enabled those miners working outside the ambit of the regular train services to throw their bikes in the guard's van for the uphill train ride, and to cycle back to Greymouth, Dunollie or Runanga under their own steam.

This was a genuine working railway. There was even a night train for miners changing shifts at midnight. This service was tagged the 'Paddy Webb' or 'Bob Semple', after coalminers who had graduated to the status of Cabinet Minister in the first Labour Government in 1935. The West Coast had always operated under its own localised imperatives. We had heard tales of six o'clock closing not counting a jot down here. Pubs waived the regulation to cater for the likes of Rewanui miners who were just as thirsty after the late-night shift as daytime workers. It wasn't just a matter of outpost defiance. The advent of ten o'clock closing in 1967 was of little consequence to the late-shift miners and Greymouth publicans.

Up in the mist at Rewanui station, with the rain easing, the engine disconnected and realigned itself at the head of the return train. The fresh miners filed off the train. Soon another shift, their onerous day underground done, shambled on to the return service as the skies really opened up. The whistle blasted and soon we were edging back down the Incline, through the soaked bush, along the perilous cutting at the edge of the cliff face. Just this side of Dunollie we made an unscheduled stop. The rain pummelled the train. The runoff created rivulets in the line-side ballast. Not surprisingly, there had been the threat of a culvert washout further down the track.

As we sat immobilised several miners — the Dunollie and Runanga contingent — left the train and walked down the waterlogged embankment to their homes. Eventually the return wet-timer eased forward past the suspect culvert gushing with runoff from the mountains, through Dunollie and Runanga and across the Grey River which was now oozing across the old S-shaped bridge.

Off to the west the Tasman crashed on the bar of the river. A small cleft of blue sky hovered above the horizon, and the rain finally eased to a mid-winter drizzle. We had one more night in the hotel over the road from the station before taking the railcar back to Christchurch in the morning.

Without really being caught out in the rain, we were, almost by a process of osmosis, wet through. That qualified us, we figured, to hunch around the horseshoe bar with the drenched miners off the Rewanui train. We were beginning to feel like part of the mildewed furniture. The miners shuffled aside and allowed us to take up station at the bar. That wouldn't have happened 24 hours earlier.

We might not have descended into the bowels of the Paparoa Ranges to work the depleting coal faces. We might not have put our lives on the line in that sense. But we had taken the time to share a unique rail experience with the West Coast weather at its worst (a day after we hightailed it out of there on the east-bound railcar, the Grey burst its banks and inundated Greymouth). And in a sense we had put something on the line — the Rewanui Incline — at a time when the Grey River threatened and the line had been all but washed out.

In 2007, we taste another slice of West Coast railwayana — the tourist attraction known as Shantytown. The sun is shining and the bush-railway that departs from the faithfully restored Shantytown station sways through the way things used to be. This journey is little more than a two-kilometre round trip past gold panning and sawmilling operations before returning to a replica West Coast settlement from the old days. A gem hall, an 1865 church, printing shop, hospital and stores complement the setting as the 1887 'Kaitangata' steam engine returns the bush train to the station. There is even provision for a contemplative beer in the saloon of a restored West Coast hotel before we continue on our way.

Shantytown is an evocative experience, but the epitome of working West Coast train experiences will always be the unscheduled yet dramatic foray up the Rewanui Incline on a very wet winter's day in 1971. Although the workers' trains ceased operation in 1984 when the mines ran out of coal, tourist trains continued to ply the Rewanui Incline as more visitors became aware of the dramatic scenery and gritty character of the Incline.

In 2007 the sparkling Greymouth weather couldn't be more different, as we are uplifted by our friends and ferried south to Kumara.

In living quarters that are part-caravan and part-container box lean-to, we find a place to rest our heads before catching the TranzAlpine back to Christchurch tomorrow. As the sun, untrammelled by cloud, disappears behind the trees, certain impressions linger. The chirp of the forest, the plunking of our friend's guitar and eventually, inevitably, the sound of returning rain in the virgin bush. Off to the west a night freight, or perhaps it's just late, crawls past on its way to Hokitika. The Taramakau River bubbles along near the hills.

A shivering realisation that we've never been here before and will probably never be here again, is sobering, even as we begin plotting our escape on the next TranzAlpine out of town. A shivering realisation too that it's bloody cold out here on the exposed deck, where the sandflies are having a field day. Our friends have jacked us up a couple of army surplus camp stretchers which tend to collapse when you so much as stir. In the end we abandon sleep and sing a few more songs. 'It takes a lot to laugh, it takes a train to cry' is the last one we sing, inspired entirely by the TranzAlpine.

I doubt very much if we would have made friends with the West Coast girls (they intend sending Christmas cards) without the incubating, inspiring TranzAlpine train. I still intend writing to Will and Barney, the Americans, but have the feeling I probably won't. Our trip back to Christchurch is more mundane. Perhaps we have been peopled and sceneried out.

It is true that a train, in New Zealand, has the potential to bring you into contact with friends you never thought you could make. Through sharing a glimpse of paradise a certain bond develops. The TranzAlpine's passage leaves you with many memories and the knowledge that you have enjoyed the journey with soulmates. It's a train that turns a dream into reality.

⑤ THE MARITIME EXPRESS: THE TRANZCOASTAL

CHRISTCHURCH TO PICTON

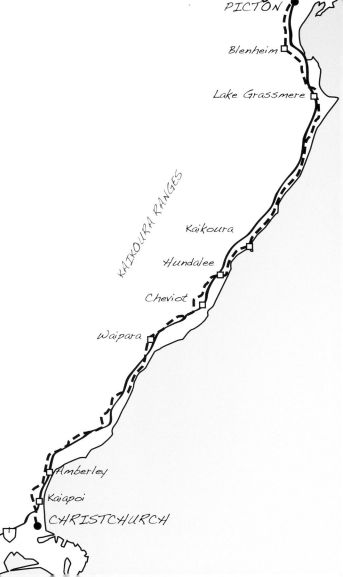

PICTON

Blenheim

Lake Grassmere

KAIKOURA RANGES

Kaikoura

Hundalee

Cheviot

Waipara

Amberley

Kaiapoi

CHRISTCHURCH

After the mesmeric coast-to-coast TranzAlpine and the step back in time on the West Coast we feel it only prudent to take a day out in Christchurch before catching the TranzCoastal up the Main North Line to Picton. No point in risking sensory overload.

Besides, Christchurch is an attractive city with a strong sense of identity. It can be preciously conservative at times. In spite — or perhaps because — of the city's buttoned-down mentality, the Wizard, an eccentric exhibitionist who used to present his version of existence from a soapbox in Cathedral Square, became not only a tourist attraction but also a virtual town father.

Christchurch used to pulsate with trains. Nowadays it has a tram, a boutique operation that trundles around the inner city. Unlike Auckland and Wellington, the city no longer has a suburban rail network. When you look at the layout of the place and the existing freight rail network, you have to ask why. A passenger service to and from Lyttleton, utilising the Lyttleton Tunnel, could serve the south-east. Trains to Rangiora in the north and Rolleston in the south would complete a three-pronged suburban network. Even a destination point some way up the Midland Line, beyond Rolleston, would serve a purpose, making it a four-way web.

Perhaps it's the right time to foist the notion of a suburban rail network on Christchurch. Before traffic gridlock arrives and the city's many cyclists find themselves shunted aside.

New Zealanders have to be hit with a good idea before they've had time to think of the reasons why it might not work. It's a cussed, down-under version of Murphy's Law, and although the Irish would take to the idea, you figure that Christchurch folk might be inclined to go for a rail option only if they're reminded of the plight of Auckland. (It's the South Island versus North Island rivalry).

Derek, an accountant we encounter on the Christchurch tram, is ready for change. He actually commutes occasionally between his home in Hereford Street and office, off Cathedral Square, by tourist tram. It costs him an arm and a leg and in truth he'd get there almost as quickly on foot, but there's a principle at stake. Derek is hankering after a Christchurch with a transport grid that doesn't rely on motor vehicles or wind-lashed bicycles. And he doesn't see why, in this day and age, he should walk. One day he'd like to live in the foothills of the Southern Alps and be able to commute by train to Cathedral Square, or as near as hell as you can get.

If there are more Dereks out there Christchurch might just be the urban centre where a subtle mind-shift, as unobtrusive as the coupling of carriages, could occur.

PREVIOUS PAGE Rail, road, mountains and sea. Key ingredients of the TranzCoastal's environment are represented here.

And it would not represent a total denial of the whims of vehicle owners. After the train there would still be the opportunity to surge out of suburban station car parks. Fendalton tractors and Bryndwr beamers would still be required to link the lines with suburban reaches beyond the train routes.

We suggest to Derek, as he climbs down from the tram in Hereford Street, that such musings may come to pass. After all, Christchurch as a potential rail hub has history on its side.

It is significant that two of New Zealand's three long-distance trains leave from the Canterbury city. And New Zealand's first stretch of line to use locomotives was the 6.8-kilometre Christchurch to Ferrymead link back in 1863. Ferrymead was a temporary port in the years before the wharves at Lyttelton could be accessed by rail (necessitating a 2.6-kilometre tunnel, opened in 1867). Obviously, Christchurch has a distinctive rail past, a fact that is celebrated at the Ferrymead Historic Park. If you have an hour or two up your sleeve the Ferrymead complex, located close to the Heathcote River Estuary, is a treasure-trove of transport memorabilia. The Ferrymead Railway, an integral part of the complex, provides train and tram rides when operating along two kilometres of track that connects with the Christchurch to Lyttelton line. The New Zealand National Railway Museum is also located within the precincts of the park, which can be accessed by travelling towards the suburb of Sumner.

As well as the operating Ferrymead Railway there is a functional electric tramway with trams from different municipal organisations, several restored steam locos and vintage passenger cars, preserved aircraft, a hall containing vintage fire trucks and a brilliantly laid out old-time village.

An organisation known as the Diesel Traction Group is also based at Ferrymead and their restored diesel locomotives are occasionally used to pull Ferrymead Railway trains.

It comes as a surprise to learn that the route of the TranzCoastal along the South Island's Main North Line was not opened until 1945. It carried the unflattering tag, waved the unflattering flag, of being the most protracted railway construction project in New Zealand rail history. The line had begun snaking north from Christchurch as long ago as 1871.

By 1876 the line had reached Amberley, some 50 km from Addington. During the following years its passage was delayed by bickering among vested interests regarding the most appropriate route to the north. A central route that would see the rail serve Nelson and the West Coast was lobbied for, while proponents of the coastal alternative — the course of today's railway — were often shunted into the background. However, when it was determined that the coastal route was some 60 km shorter than the central option, its highest point 700 m lower and the fact that it traversed more agricultural and rural properties, the gavel fell in its favour.

Not that the decision led to a frenzy of construction activity. By now the depression of the 1880s had hit and railway building in general came to a halt. Eventually, in 1912, the line had crawled as far as Parnassus, 133 km from Christchurch, but before it could go much further

Not that I particularly liked cheese, not back then anyway. All that blue vein stuff and a holey, grey goat's milk job that looked like stoat's brains.

the outbreak of World War 1, with its demands on manpower and building materials, caused further delay.

Procrastination, based on the exorbitant costs of the link, dragged the argument into the 1930s. At that point global issues intervened again in the shape of the Great Depression. Funds were not available for further expansion.

At the other end of the route a line from Picton to Blenheim in Marlborough had become operational in 1875, but similar problems were to affect the northern link. In the early 1900s work commenced in a southerly direction from Blenheim and by 1915 the line had reached Wharanui on the coast, 90 km south of Picton. Here, development stalled because of World War 1 and Wharanui, like Parnassus in the south, became the terminus and railhead.

It took the election of the first Labour Government in 1935 to reinstate development of the line. Good progress was made in the years leading up to World War II but the privations of war led to familiar delays. Eventually, the final spike in the link between north and south was driven near Kaikoura in September 1945, and the official opening of the line took place in December of that year.

It's now 2007 and the current passenger service on the line — in fact the only one — is getting ready to depart Christchurch, heading north. The TranzCoastal, run these days by Toll Rail, has developed a reputation as one of the most picturesque rail journeys with an ocean aspect, and I approach Carriage C with anticipation and a sharp sprint. It leaves reasonably early and I'm a late riser. Before I've even settled in my seat a red-faced middle-aged man starts talking. He is off to Marlborough to see his friend Maria, a fellow wine buff.

'Maria says the first time she saw me, I had over-imbibed at a wine and cheese evening — there was too much wine and not enough cheese, apparently. Not that I particularly liked cheese, not back then anyway. All that blue vein stuff and a holey, grey goat's milk job that looked like stoat's brains. Blue vein was like eating varicose veins when your system was used to the mopping-up properties of fish and chips. And some of the wine was powerful in those days of fortified Henderson red.'

I settle in my seat as the TranzCoastal starts moving. My travelling companion continues talking.

'After the Cold Duck, that was me done for the evening. I was snoring loudly in the back of the car when Maria was introduced to me. I'd like to think I shook her hand. At least I'd had the decency to sneak away and hide my disgrace. Shame it was the wrong car, that's all. But it was Maria's. She wouldn't be pressing charges. I mean, there are significant similarities between a Volkswagen Beetle and a Fiat Bambina at two in the morning.'

Now, in 2007, as the TranzCoastal angles out of Addington Station, ruddy-faced Warren is striking out again on the wine trail, through Marlborough where the finest white wines flourish. Rough reds are part of a tough past. One of the briefs of the TranzCoastal now is to carry wine pilgrims to Blenheim and beyond in pursuit of the perfect Sauvignon Blanc. Great white hunters graze, elaborately hatted against the perishing sun, appropriately garbed in the knowledge that you never know what sort of wildlife you may stumble upon — literally. There could be a towering lawyer loping among the vines; fully developed rednecks from rural Canterbury identifiable by their distinctive straw boaters; female Wellington CEOs in wearable art . . .

Warren will be meeting up with Maria at Blenheim, completing a wine cycle that extends all the way back to the days when Blackberry Nip could nip you in the bud. After his initial tirade Warren loses himself in wine brochures and the *Wine Atlas of New Zealand*, a heavy tome that keeps falling off his lap. The train, as smooth as a good Marlborough Sav B, slips out of the station heading north.

The TranzCoastal leaves these days from the avant garde Addington Station. Don't know how I feel about that. When I first came to Christchurch in the late 1960s to sample local rail services, my first experience of the old Moorhouse Street Station was reassuring. It was a real railway station. The old building now houses cinemas and other inappropriate functions. There might even be a church of sorts in there.

The TranzCoastal is virtually full as we gather speed. There is no doubting the fact that the modern train is far more salubrious than the old, faded red railcar. There is a steadiness of gait, a sense of space not associated with the old service, and a hum of expectation among the passengers compared to a certain dourness back in 1967, when I first travelled on this line.

We pass through Riccarton, Fendalton, Bryndwr and Papanui as passengers, many of them foreign tourists, settle to the rhythm of the train. This is the middle-class route out of town. Stately homes, rambling gardens. Fendalton has been described as the Remuera of the south. If tourists harbour any notions of New Zealand still being some sort of egalitarian paradise, they will be thinking twice as the train speeds through the privileged backyards of North Christchurch.

Papanui Station now houses a restaurant. I recently dined in its delightfully refurbished chambers. A friend of the family was the chef and his crayfish bisque followed by venison provençal were only matched for appeal by the sudden rush and vibration as first a northbound freight train and, between dessert and coffee, the southbound TranzCoastal rocketed through.

I don't know if Papanui was ever a refreshment stop in the old days. Being so close to the city it probably wasn't. But back then trains seemed slower, appetites keener, and there were more services, including a suburban link that stopped everywhere on its way to and from Rangiora. If Papanui had been a refreshment stop it was hard not to set the rock cakes, pies, sandwiches and slabs of fruit cake of old against the 'fine dining' fare we sampled at the station restaurant, washed down by a risqué Riesling with oak overtones and mildly assertive mood swings.

For all that the ramble through the northern suburbs is easy on the eye. After the rugged, down-home ambience of many West Coast settlements, the plush, comfortable

A blink and you miss something. The spectacular scenery becomes more apparent as the TranzCoastal heads north.

and extremely English two-storeyed houses, set in carefully manicured grounds, serve to remind travellers that pockets of New Zealand owe much to our English heritage. During the first 20 km of the TranzCoastal journey English travellers must feel right at home.

Kaiapoi, north of Christchurch, lies just the other side of the Waimakariri River. There was a time when this was a corner of the North Canterbury countryside. In fact even the suburb of Styx was regarded as 'out in the sticks'. Perhaps that's how its name originated, with a few affectations. Urban development has made its mark. Kaiapoi was more likely a refreshment stop at one time. Now the TranzCoastal stops long enough to pick up passengers and affords an Indian gentleman the chance to hop out onto the platform and huff and puff on a fag like the big bad wolf. Not that he has the blessing of the train staff. He is soon shunted back on the train, flicking his half-smoked cigarette under the wheels of the carriage.

As the TranzCoastal heads inland across the remnants of the Canterbury Plains towards Rangiora the Indian man swears that the smoking ban would never happen on Indian Railways. I suggest that in his country he could repair to the carriage roof for a quick drag. I immediately regret my throwaway remark, waiting for the retort of an offended man. Instead he flashes a knowing smile and introduces himself as Ramesh. Ramesh is a school teacher in Madras, a smoker, and a fervent fan of rail travel. More than anything I am relieved to find he is a man of some humour, although the woman standing next to us gives me a withering stare that suggests if the victim of such a racist comment does not take the matter higher, she will

almost certainly do so. However, it seems I've earned the withering stare simply because I unwittingly jumped the queue to the buffet counter.

As we find a seat towards the rear of the train, amid a gaggle of texting young Kiwis, Ramesh's world vision becomes clearer.

'I know I am extremely lucky. Most of my fellow countrymen would never get the chance to travel like this, not even on the roof of the TranzCoastal.'

His distinctive cackle between gulps of coffee is reassuring. Suddenly a long-limbed adolescent extends his legs across the aisle towards us, resting his exposed, pimply extremities almost in our laps. It is an ungainly gesture.

'Would you do that at home?' Ramesh barks in his best schoolteacher manner.

'Yeah.'

'Well perhaps that's where you should confine such behaviour.'

The adolescent and his companions, after considering fight or flight, opt staunchly for the latter. As they shamble out of the carriage, variously sending text messages, slugging back bottled water or donning dark glasses, Ramesh rolls his eyes.

One good thing that emerges from the unusual exchange in the end carriage is that we now have total, if temporary, ownership of the rear of the train. Magnificent views of the green North Canterbury farmlands and river valleys fill the carriage. Braided rivers and long rail bridges provide contrast.

The rivers may be braided and trickling but come the rains and snow-melt in the ranges, often at the same time,

they will need every inch of their watercourses to cope with the deluge.

I remember travelling to and from Christchurch in 1989 and on the way down the braided rivers of North Canterbury were largely bereft of water. A week later on the return journey, the Ashley River just out of Rangiora was so engorged with flood waters the train had to inch its way across the river bridge with rapids forming as the surge crested the railway lines themselves. My two young kids had been very concerned at the water level. I wasn't completely relaxed either, but the train staff reckoned such a crossing was par for the course at various times of the year. Funnily enough, it only seemed to be the Ashley River that was chock-full.

The Ashley River also features in New Zealand Rail folklore. There was a popular pub located close to the Ashley River bridge in the old days and, taking advantage of the fact that they were out of range and beyond immediate censure by rail bosses, train drivers, firemen and guards reported delays because of burst air hoses on the bridge. A brief scramble down the embankment would see the crew passing time in the pub, while their train, the only one occupying an infrequently used line, waited patiently.

As Christchurch becomes North Canterbury and the plains merge with the green-brown hills to the north, Ramesh becomes animated by the number of SUV-vehicles on the roads that shadow the TranzCoastal's route. Quite reasonably, he wants to know if the 'off-road' vehicles intend, in fact, to go off-road and seek out mountains like Sir Edward Hillary (I remind him that it is Sir Edmund). Perhaps they intend to bounce up the river beds in search of deer, or wild pig? As the train swings back towards Amberley, I acknowledge that most such vehicles on the highway are point A to B carriers of kids, families, grandparents, dogs.

'I bet they're allowed to smoke in those things.' Ramesh is obviously hankering after a cigarette.

Beyond Amberley the land closes in a bit and we begin to climb. Soon we reach Waipara, which used to be the junction point with the old Waiau Branch. It now provides the gateway for the vintage Weka Pass Railway.

The Waipara Valley is one of New Zealand's fastest-developing wine districts and attracts a growing number of visitors to sample the local pinot noir, riesling, chardonnay and sauvignon blanc.

Waipara the settlement is a prominent highway junction point, but there's nothing much in the way of accommodation. Except for Waipara Sleepers, a backpacker accommodation situation that features old railway guards' vans lovingly converted into dormitories and an ancient New Zealand Rail station which provides the setting for the typical bustling backpacker kitchen. Waipara Sleepers complements the Weka Pass Railway in giving Waipara and the Waipara Valley a distinctive rail ambience.

As the TranzCoastal passes through the oddly named Spye, the highest point between Bluff and Picton, we are definitely climbing. The plains are long gone. The off-roaders out the window recede, although trucks are now banking up, thwarted by the rising gradient.

Traversing the picturesque Hurunui River Gorge adds to the feeling of serenity. The valley is variously grass green with tufts of brown and yellow. The hills, folding

OPPOSITE Well-ordered crops form patterns on the flats near Waipara.

back, range through several shades of deeper green until the distant foothills become grey-blue, merging with the patchy sky.

There is little inkling of what lies ahead scenically as the TranzCoastal continues northward. The plains have given way to gently rolling sheep country. Foothills occasionally part, revealing mountains off on the hazy horizon. After a clear early morning, cloud banks are beginning to cluster. Showers are forecast further on up the coast. The roar of steel on suspended steel continues to punctuate the easy cadence of the train, as long rail bridges cross the wide, braided rivers near their communion with the Pacific Ocean. We've already crossed the Waimakariri, Ashley and Kowai. Soon we'll encounter the Waiau and Conway.

Cheviot, the only settlement of significance between Waipara and Kaikoura, is located some distance from the TranzCoastal's passage. The nearest station is the oddly named Phoebe. Yet Cheviot and its district was the scene of critical change in the way New Zealanders reapportioned land holdings. In the early years of European settlement, in Cheviot and its hinterland, vast estates in relatively few hands predominated. In 1893 Sir John McKenzie, a Cabinet Minister, divided the estates into smaller holdings so the number of locals able to work and live off the land expanded from 80 to 650. McKenzie's action, one whose time had come, was applied throughout New Zealand in an early display of Kiwi egalitarianism.

One of the highlights of train travel in New Zealand occurs when the TranzCoastal reaches the coast not far from Hundalee. Bodies of water bode well. When the commuter service from Wellington breaches the Rimutaka Tunnel, opening out on to the vast expanse of Lake Wairarapa, the spirit soars. When the Overlander surreptitiously snuggles up to the Waikato River on its long journey north, the silent, slow waters add an entirely different dimension to the journey.

So it is with the northbound TranzCoastal when it leaves the landlocked Canterbury-Marlborough hinterland behind. Passengers stop talking. Cameras and camcorders start clicking and whirring. The Pacific Ocean opens out in a truly spectacular display of maritime railway magnificence. As a nation we hanker after the comforting notion that we are never too far from the ocean at any given place or time. From Oaro north the route of the train provides evidence of our 'islander' status: miles of open ocean.

If you had poor sea legs, the TranzCoastal, as it shadows the Pacific coast, might trigger a bout of nausea. On a wild day with sea spray splattering the carriage windows, the illusion might be more pronounced. On most days, given the equitable climate in this corner of the country, the ocean is as gentle as a lamb. The even camber of the train, one of rail travel's most attractive features, keeps all but the most sensitive of stomachs settled.

Seemingly on cue, sudden southerly squalls assail the train, sending spray splattering against the carriage windows while a million whitecaps fleck the Pacific all the way to the far horizon. A global sense of vastness and New Zealand's unique position in the southern ocean is a thought-provoking yet exhilarating aspect of travelling up this long and lonely coastline.

As the train prepares to stop at Kaikoura, the whale-watch capital of New Zealand, Ramesh hovers in the

OPPOSITE Kaikoura, the town that went from plundering whales to watching them, all in the name of commerce.

vestibule wiith a packet of Pall Mall at the ready. Despite the squalls he is able to polish off three cigarettes on the platform, hunched over, his back to the southerly. While he is thus detained a woman called Polly takes a seat in our enclosure. Dishevelled by the wind, she is pleased to be in the toasty warmth of the carriage. She is one of those friendly, old-fashioned South Islanders, 60ish and likely, in another era, to be knitting by now.

Kaikoura used to be a quiet backwater, located along a coastal ribbon that you would occasionally sight from the deck of the ferry that ran between Wellington and Christchurch. Goose Bay, south of Kaikoura, was a shore whaling station in the early days of European settlement. Kaikoura was also associated with early whaling stations, but historically it is more significant for being the place where the South Island Main North railway line was completed. A ceremony marking the event was enacted at the Kaikoura station, where a plaque not only celebrates the link's completion but also honours the eight rail construction workers who lost their lives during the building of the railway.

The line was the last trunk railway to be completed in New Zealand, and Kaikoura Station was the final refreshment stop on the New Zealand rail network until the introduction of the onboard buffet of the Coastal Pacific Express, the forerunner of today's TranzCoastal, in 1988. I can recall an uncharacteristically lukewarm cup of coffee and a stiffened, upturned ham sandwich during the course of a railcar journey up the Main North Line in 1971. I was hoping for a bowl of steaming lobster thermador, or perhaps a bite of crayfish tails. At school we learned that Kaikoura meant crayfish meal.

Behind the town lie two mountain ranges, the nearer Seaward Kaikouras and the far Inland Kaikouras. Brian Ford, a strong-running truck driver from Kaikoura, became an All Black in the 1970s. He started out playing for Canterbury, before representing his country on behalf of the humble Marlborough Union. Ford didn't move base. The rugby hierarchy simply changed the boundary line between Canterbury and Marlborough, which rendered Kaikoura a Marlborough satellite. Apart from such details Kaikoura did not loom large in earlier decades.

Then local entrepreneurs cottoned on to the notion of reinventing Kaikoura as a marine life mecca. Whales and dolphins had always gallivanted in the placid bay. Seals too, long-time Kaikoura residents, fitted the new tourism model. The town was largely made over, with trendy cafés and shops reflecting the reinvention. Scenically it is one of New Zealand's prettiest towns and many of its 3000-plus inhabitants owe their new lease of life to the creatures of the sea. Whales, in particular, lead the way, just as they did when Kaikoura was becoming established as a settlement. Back then whales were hunted down and drawn and quartered in shore whaling operations that continued into the twentieth century, until such activities ceased in 1922. Now tourists merely watch the whales from boats, and further observe the dolphins and seals, while continuing to eat crayfish and other abundant sea life.

Kaikoura looks like an attractive stopping-over location. Perhaps next time. Meanwhile as the Tranz-Coastal heads out of Kaikoura our attention turns to our new travelling companion.

OPPOSITE Concrete viaducts are a feature of the Main North Line, testimony to the fact that the line was the final New Zealand main route to be completed.

Polly put the kettle on, so she reckons. Still does at home of course. She recalls with affection the Kaikoura refreshment rooms of the 1950s when, as a young woman, she helped prepare the cups of tea and coffee for thirsty travellers. Polly's been retired for a few years now. She and her late husband used to run an old-fashioned tearooms in Kaikoura's main street, applying the experience gained while working for New Zealand Railways.

Meanwhile as the ocean aspect continues to beguile, Polly tells us of her downer on the new-fangled coffee bars, or cafés as they call them. How suddenly everyone is going ga-ga over coffee again. It's a second turn of the wheel, or coffee grinder, Polly reckons, harking back to phase one of the caffeine craze which, to all intents and purposes, died a death in the 1970s. She may have a valid point but it's hard to remain focused on the issue with the train stretching out over the brilliantly braided Hapuku River, its shingle and scrubby bush forming patterns that could have inspired those generous patched cardigans and jerseys that knitting nanas clacked into life on the old trains. Off to the west the snow-flecked Seaward Kaikouras, set now against a clearing deep blue sky, no doubt also provided input into the woolly tableaux. Cardies aside, the sheer magnificence of the landscape distracts us from our conversation.

A colourful feature of the TranzCoastal's route north of Kaikoura is the gypsy-like community of caravan takeaway outlets and humble shacks that highlight their food wares, often fruits of the sea, in painted sign language that says less about local dialects than about the failure of the New Zealand education system. As the train rattles past, signs advertise 'Deep fried muscles', 'Cheese and union sandwiches', 'Dognuts'.

There's no doubting the preponderance of seafood and offerings from deep-fry vats, but there is a case for doubting the spelling skills of Marlborough food vendors. Or are they from North Canterbury?

As the train heads towards Clarence, still hugging the spectacular, hemmed-in coast, you wonder about the effect of such isolation.

Train drivers along the line sometimes stop at lonely outposts like Rakautara to buy crayfish. It seems significant that the signal to do so is the presence of a faded pink shed on the beach rim. Pidgin English signs are not needed. Colours are the train drivers' identification markers. Red, green and amber signal lights — and pink sheds — see the train safely through. The line was always a lonely, unencumbered one. In the days — or nights — of the 'cabbage train', a mixed service that derived its name from its perishable cargo of fresh produce destined for points north, it was possible to count the number of trains on the fingers of one hand.

The weather clears as the train continues along the coast heading north. The ocean dazzles. You can sense the invigorating presence of the sea, although Ramesh nods off not long after the TranzCoastal crosses the Hapuku River. Perhaps it's a Kiwi thing. Polly goes one better, and gets off at Wharanui.

Russ and I, stultified to a certain extent by the scenic grandeur, and feeling liberated in a funny way by Polly's departure, decide to wander aft to the backpackers' carriage, the one with smaller, traditional windows.

Expecting to find a gaggle of young tourists with knobbly knees and heads adorned with backwards baseball caps and sunglasses, we find instead history repeating itself. Back in 1997, on an earlier pilgrimage, we stumbled on a carriage full of celebrating middle-aged lawn bowlers on their way back to Blenheim. Now, in 2007, we find a carriage-worth of dart players from Picton who have scooped the pool in Kaikoura. We suggest that they may have taken out the top prize in a whale-riding rodeo, the next big thing on the adrenaline-tourist calendar.

In terms of railway history it's the closest we've come to the late-1970s booze-ups on the Auckland to Wellington Express. Times have changed though. Everyone is drinking wine, even the men, some of whom look like ageing prop forwards. Sauvignon Blanc, Chardonnay — the local product. The clunk of brown beer bottles had been replaced by the clink of wine miniatures from the buffet.

As the train at last curves away from the coast, the Picton darters suddenly voice an affirmation in unison, before merging in the corridor to hug one another. As mass clinches go it's as tight as a King Country scrum. Their weird chant is followed by a mid-corridor scrum, half haka, half highland fling, at which point we retreat.

As the train crawls along the causeway through the salt works of Lake Grassmere, Warren, his wine trail game plan in place, has begun to prepare for de-training, although we are miles from Blenheim. Perhaps it's a good game plan.

Clarence River, with its folklore relating to the wreck of the *Taiaroa*, when 34 lives were lost in 1886, Kekerengu, Wharanui and the 'Tar Barrel' Tunnel, which takes the line under the highway and away from the coast, have

already passed as we settle back into our seats.

Leaving the coast is a time of mourning. You always knew the time would come. But like any such loss, the crossing of the Rubicon is hard to take.

Not long after the train leaves the ocean and heads inland, I nod off. They reckon exposure to the ocean can leave you sleepy and soporific. Seddon, Ward and Blenheim pass in a blur.

While I am half-snoozing the TranzCoastal passes through some of the more interesting inland settlements. Ward used to be a typically bustling, sheep-oriented town and station. Livestock handling in 1946 saw 13,383 sheep, 217 cattle, nine horses and 18 pigs pass through. Bearing in mind that the line was opened just the year before, the number of humans can only be guessed at, but no doubt it was significant.

My first journey through Ward occurred when Vulcan railcars were still running. One of the earliest promised consignments of Vulcan railcars never made it to New Zealand. The ship carrying the doomed vehicle was torpedoed during World War II and the railcar now lies on the ocean bed somewhere between the Vulcan works in England and its intended New Zealand destination.

Lake Grassmere is one of the most unusual rail passages on the New Zealand system. The line runs through what is basically a salt farm, where commercial salt is harvested on the back of high sunshine hours, hastening evaporation of salt water, and easy access to the sea. Boisterous north-westerly winds aid the evaporation process in a memorable rail setting that, since 1943, has seen Lake Grassmere become the principal producer

The Seddon War Memorial close to the Seddon railway station.

OPPOSITE At times you could be forgiven for thinking you were on a boat. The view from the TranzCoastal as the line hugs the coast.

A mound of salt creates a diversion as the train encounters Lake Grassmere near Clifford Bay.

The brown reaches beyond Seddon have me stirring, and the climb up through the Dashwood Pass before descending on a long, mesmerising horseshoe curve. Seddon and Ward were named after former New Zealand Prime Ministers. I half expect the next town to be called Muldoon.

Seddon, on the banks of Starborough Creek, a feeder stream of the Awatere River, has been resurrected to a certain extent by the general resurgence of Blenheim, a few kilometres to the north. Viticulture is creeping its way south, along with the attendant tourism factor. The Seddon railway station, closed in a mean gesture by NZ Rail in 1987, has been rescued and renovated by well-intentioned privateers to the extent that it now boasts a café, wineshop and art gallery within its traditional railway station precincts. Some passengers alight at Seddon simply to take in the ambience of the station.

Ramesh begins to come around as the TranzCoastal drifts along the plains prior to pulling into Blenheim. Fag-stop city as far as Ramesh is concerned, and he dashes away to do his 'puffing billy' impersonation. Warren, after preparing to alight almost an hour earlier, makes an ungainly exit, trailing unfurled brochures and struggling manfully with a large rucksack that throws him off course several times.

Outside, vineyards and wineries stretch to the heat-hazy horizon. Warren won't be short of a drop.

Blenheim used to present as a small, sun-drenched settlement, off the beaten track, until the inter-island ferries began linking Wellington with Picton at the base of Queen Charlotte Sound. Then viticulture and

of commercial salt in New Zealand. The passage of the TranzCoastal through the salt mountains keeps the pecker up once the picturesque coast has been relinquished. The pink algal pigmentation that sometimes arises in the manmade lake is similar in colour to the pink beachside shack back down the line at Rakautara, where crayfish are available to train drivers.

Then come the faded hills of northern Marlborough.

wine production arrived, and the attendant prestige and tourism, and Blenheim blew out, population-wise, to about 27,000.

All the while of course it remained located on the Main North Line between Christchurch and Picton. The early expresses, the 'cabbage' mixed trains, the Vulcan railcars and now the TranzCoastal have touched base with Blenheim, with its distinctive stately 1906 wooden station, which in recent years was shunted 70 metres to provide space for a car park.

Someone suggested, somewhat unfairly, that if Blenheim lost all its grapevines there'd be little reason to stop over in the Marlborough 'capital'. It used to be infamous for flooding in early days when the overflow from the Wairau River to the north cascaded through the low-lying town. Local politics and diversion schemes dealt to that problem. Later it became a ho-hum agricultural service centre, admittedly blessed with high sunshine hours. Then, as a minor-division, off-the-beaten-track rugby provincial headquarters, it helped orchestrate the winning of the Ranfurly Shield, symbol of provincial rugby supremacy in a rugby-besotted land.

Perhaps it was the presence of the Ranfurly Shield, but soon Blenheimers were re-evaluating their place in the scheme of things. The planting of vineyards, taking advantage of appropriate soils and those precious sunshine hours, transformed the former sleepy hollow. Blenheim, the capital of Marlborough wine country, now boasts the best Sauvignon Blanc in the world and, with 40 percent of the New Zealand grape harvest, has pipped Hawke's Bay as the country's leading bulk producer of grapes.

Many TranzCoastal passengers, apart from Warren — in fact as far apart as possible — alight at Blenheim to take up wine trail options. Once their wine palate has been sated, and the invigorating walks in the Richmond Ranges have cleared heads, and the burgeoning restaurant and nightlife scene has had a decent seeing-to, such travellers will take the next day's TranzCoastal that climbs out of the valley and heads through the hills towards Picton.

Beyond Grovetown and Spring Creek, we encounter hillsides flecked with forest. The small settlement of Tuamarina is notable for its cheese factory and the fact that the Wairau Affray, the only armed conflict between settlers and Maori to occur in the South Island, took place nearby in 1843.

Flotsam on the road bridge supports attests to recent flooding in the foothills. The rivers are wide and braided for good reason.

The locations of Para, Koromiko and Mount Pleasant pass as the train climbs, appropriately, to Elevation. The TranzCoastal swings on to the Waitohi Viaduct, an angled approach to Picton, the northern terminus of the Main North Line.

As the train pulls into the beautifully restored Picton station, it is impossible not to be beguiled by a unique rail setting on the lip of Queen Charlotte Sound. There was a time when boat-trains across Cook Strait, between Picton and Wellington, rather like their Scandinavian equivalents linking Denmark and Sweden, were very much on the drawing board. In recent years noises have been made to the effect that Clifford Bay, around the Pacific coast, will become the new terminal.

In the meantime, as we wait for the Interislander — which berths little more than a casual saunter away or a sharp sprint if you've dallied on the platform to enjoy the station café fare while watching carriages and wagons from the North Island being bunted about by a shunting diesel — echoes of the TranzCoastal return.

Between the quiet green hills of North Canterbury and the coffee cake-hued domes of Northern Marlborough, the Pacific Ocean, with its mood-swinging weather and quaint settlements, has dominated. And a train has taken the time to thread its way through 24 tunnels, over countless bridges, and screeched around sea-lashed ramparts in the interests of getting the people north. A magical, maritime train-ride has been the bonus.

Picton is an ideal stopping-off point to explore the scenic Marlborough Sounds, many parts of which are accessible only by sea. However, Queen Charlotte Drive to the west of the town provides road access to Queen Charlotte Sound and, further on via Havelock, Pelorus Sound. Hiring a car offers the option of exploring the unique beauty of the Sounds if it suits you to delay the ferry crossing for another day.

Picton itself, with its historic, scenic and transport features is worthy of close inspection. The rail came relatively early to Picton and the Picton to Blenheim link was opened in 1875. The connection that consummated the current course of the TranzCoastal had to wait until 1945, and for that reason the notion of a scenically splendid, largely sea-girt train link has taken a while to enter the consciousness of New Zealand travellers. That may be the reason why so many foreign travellers, including chain-smoking Indian schoolteachers, take to the train link between Christchurch and Picton with barely a second thought. Kiwis are still grappling with the notion.

The Picton foreshore celebrates its maritime aspect. Old ships like the *Edwin Fox*, the last surviving vessel of the type that transported migrants to New Zealand, and the *Echo*, a schooner that was the last ship of its kind to operate commercially in local waters, play starring roles at the edge of the lapping waters of Queen Charlotte Sound.

From Picton the Interislander takes you to Wellington. New Zealand's capital will be the starting point for the North Island leg of this rail jaunt from south to north. But before we set out on that journey, a brief digression takes us along a restored branch line that missed its chance long ago to provide the main route north to Blenheim.

⑥ THE FROG ROCK FLYER: THE WEKA PASS RAILWAY

WAIPARA TO WAIKARI

The Weka Pass Railway took shape on the initial 13 km of what was once the Waiau Branch in North Canterbury. From Waipara, the junction point with the main north line to Picton, the Weka Pass railway climbs up through the Weka Pass, past strange limestone configurations, before terminating its journey at Waikari.

The line used to carry on as far as Waiau, nearly 67 km from Waipara. The original intention, as long ago as 1882, when the first section to Waikari was opened, was to extend the inland line beyond Waiau all the way to Blenheim. However, the coastal route eventually gained favour, condemning the Weka Pass route to branch-line status.

It was a fully fledged main line in the early days, with all the trappings. Waipara, Culverden and Waiau were all locomotive depots. Four daily return trains ran on the section between Culverden and Christchurch. With the extension to Waiau complete, further trains were added including two daily passenger trains serving Culverden. It was a lively railway environment. Some of the old-fashioned romance of the railways must have been in the air as at one stage travellers took the train as far as Culverden, preparatory to catching a linking bus to Hanmer Springs. Shades almost of the romantic Rotorua Express that carried the Auckland 'drinkies' set to take the waters and whatever else was on offer in the tourist town of Rotorua.

Two trains a day still operated on the line in 1968, by which time diesel engines were de rigueur. At this stage the line was sustained by general goods and the annual mustering of stock on the huge Molesworth Station, which utilised the rail to transport beasts from Culverden to the saleyards at Addington, Christchurch. At a time when livestock numbers on similar rural lines had faded significantly, several specially appointed stock trains kept this line open.

Then nature threw the branch an additional lifeline. A ferocious storm in 1975 bowled much of nearby Balmoral State Forest and for over two years regular log trains transported the sudden windfall down the branch and on to Timaru where the logs were shipped out to Japan.

Once the logs had gone, closure proceeded, but not until a union black ban had been placed on the removal of the tracks, during which time dedicated locals and outside rail enthusiasts were able to set up the Weka Pass Railway Society and purchase the tracks from Waipara to the Waikari Road crossing.

PREVIOUS PAGE On a chilly April morning engine A 428 attracts Weka Pass Railway travellers as much for the warmth, as the pied piper aspect of steam engines.

After 1978 the lines rusted and the weeds encroached. The sight of trains west of Waipara became a thing of the past — until the Weka Pass railway aficionados assembled. Soon the ghostly shrill of steam engine whistles and the once-familiar clatter of carriages and wagons over refurbished track would return to the North Canterbury hills.

To this end, steam locomotive A428, generously donated by a preservationist in Greymouth, was placed on the block for restoration. Five years later it was ready. The 13 kilometres of track between Waipara and Waikari was rebuilt, utilising existing New Zealand Rail embankments. The station from Mina, a little further north, was transported, renovated and renamed Glenmark. The station building from Hundalee that once graced the main north line was shifted to Waikari and similarly refurbished.

The Kiwi spirit had triumphed. The bureaucrats won the major battle but not the minor skirmish. The march of progress was thwarted somewhat and the outcome — the Weka Pass Railway — is a fine testament to a group of volunteers who carved out one of the most charming New Zealand train journeys and a valuable tourist attraction.

In 1995 the Rail Heritage Trust of New Zealand recognised the outstanding restoration of the two stations by granting an award of some consequence to the vintage railway.

The North Canterbury mist shrouds the setting as we approach the Weka Pass Railway in 2007. In this rural enclave it seemed appropriate to be catching a vintage train that looks like a 1930s New Zealand branch-line service. The Weka Pass Express boasts the coal-burning

motive force — A428 — and a rake of traditional rail-red carriages. There is even a time-honoured guards van bringing up the rear.

Out of the mist Weka Pass rail travellers emerge like ghosts up from the coast. The numbers are surprising. By the time A428 blasts its departure call, most carriages are full. Butting out through the fog, the train replicates the past — when train travel was often associated with dodgy weather, occasional showers, rain dumps and unscheduled mist clouds. The Weka Pass train could not have set out under more appropriate weather conditions.

Mind you, as the train stretches out along the flat,

The Weka Pass Railway, a vintage jaunt back in time, is accessible at Waipara.

Old 'railway red' carriages glowing through the mist. The 'Frog Rock Flyer' (Weka Pass Express) waits at Glenmark Station.

a photo opportunity that will produce tangible evidence that a steam-drawn re-enactment of a traditional branch-line rural service is alive and well in North Canterbury.

Arriving at Waikari, the end of the Weka Pass Railway line, is memorable too. The station overlooks the remote settlement, nestled on an embankment high above the Star and Garter pub and sundry shops and houses.

We have time for a pint and pie in the pub, clustered around a roaring fire in the bar that provides the setting for some sort of debriefing session among the local fire service volunteers. The pint is good, the pie a bit crusty, but the locals are friendly. Then it's a matter of ascending the grade back to the station, past a secondhand store, craft shops and tearooms, where young North Canterbury folk hover, before rejoining the train for the return journey. The mist has lifted and it's all downhill from here.

The ride down the line highlights the scenic setting of the railway. The curious rock formations around Frog Rock are thrust into sharper relief. Frog Rock really does look like a frog. The light-grey limestone rocks randomly aligned along the deep green flanks of Weka Pass are a distinctive landscape. Further on the Waipara Valley and its confining hills create an illusion of distance as the outlines of the new vineyards on the valley floor come into sharper focus.

A remarkably compact and authentic vintage steam train ride (diesel-hauled in times of high brushfire risk) and a fine bottle of local bubbly. Such goodies are attracting tourists in greater numbers to the Waipara hinterland. One day, one suspects, Pinot Noir will be available on the enchanting Weka Pass Railway.

past the newly-established vineyards, the sun is already poking through and as we climb into the hills the mist retires shyly behind us.

State Highway 7, the Lewis Pass road, joins the climb up through Weka Pass. Several carloads of travellers have stopped in their tracks, fascinated by the sight of a steam-hauled train fighting the grade. Some just wave at the train in the time-honoured South Island manner, others crank up cameras and video recorders as the train crests the ridge leading to the remarkable limestone outcrops at Frog Rock.

The train stops and passengers are invited to alight for

⑦ UNDER THE HILLS AND FAR AWAY: THE WAIRARAPA TRAIN

WELLINGTON TO MASTERTON

Wellington, in rail terms, is one hell of a town. The railway is taken for granted, the central railway station invariably awash with patrons. In this respect it is like no other New Zealand city. Auckland, with its dramatically increased suburban patronage centred on the new subterranean Britomart Station, processes commuters still mesmerised by the flickering lights and increased travel options. It's almost as if a brave new way of commuter travel has become both possible and beguiling. In Wellington, the rail option has always been there and commuters regard it as second nature.

PREVIOUS PAGE Making like a traditional provincial express, the Wairarapa commuter service gathers speed.

It is a pleasant surprise to learn that the train from Wellington to Wairarapa is still running. At a time when a one-off service between Auckland and Hamilton — a similar operation to the Wairarapa train, connecting a provincial city with a major conurbation — is struggling to get off the ground, the on-going popularity of the Wellington-Masterton train is surprising.

Such runs seem to be a thing of the past. The various incarnations of the Wellington to Napier, Wellington to New Plymouth, Auckland to Rotorua and Auckland to Tauranga services, to name a few, have disappeared. Wellington to Masterton appeared to be in the same category, yet here it is running five times a day there and back, six times on a Friday, twice on weekends.

The willingness of Wellingtonians to use their train services has been a significant factor in their survival. The Wairarapa service falls under the ambit of Tranz Metro, the suburban passenger operator. Many capital city workers commute from Masterton and other Wairarapa towns; the continued survival of the train should come as no surprise therefore, even with successive operators itching to slash and burn rail services in recent years.

It has been said that the looming presence of the Rimutaka Ranges, and the rail tunnel through them, has kept bums on train seats. Had there been a road tunnel as well the Wairarapa service might have dwindled and died.

But it is very much alive and kicking — a real train with a large diesel loco and lived-in sky-blue carriages. The train that leaves Wellington at 8.25 am is filling quickly despite the fact that most commuters at this time of day are coming into the city.

Suddenly it feels like the 1960s again, although as the train to Masterton pulls out of Wellington the operation is conducted just like any other suburban junket.

Soon we are gathering speed along the scenic stretch of track beside the harbour towards the Hutt Valley. Small boats bounce around in the choppy water. White caps extend to the far reaches of Eastbourne.

The train makes scheduled stops at Petone, Waterloo (the Lower Hutt rail-bus interchange hub where a station worker is suspended in a glass dome near the track to oversee the perambulations), Upper Hutt and Maymorn, before encountering the long Rimutaka Tunnel. The Hutt Valley is extensively suburbanised. State houses predominate in many pockets, but the old villas made over in centres like Petone show evidence of gentrification. Above the valley, in the Hutt hills, substantial newer homes have been built since the once essentially working-class suburbs came of age in the 1950s and 1960s.

The train gathers speed as it heads east through Epuni, Naenae, Wingate, Taita, Pomare, Manor Park and Trentham. Dark smudges on the platform disappear in a blur — the sombrely-dressed commuters massing on the suburban track platforms to catch trains heading for the corporate canyons of downtown Wellington.

The Rimutakas presented such a barrier to line builders in the early days that they opted for a revolutionary approach. Utilising a centre rail adhesion system developed by English engineer, John Barraclough Fell, a steep incline on the Wairarapa side was the only solution at the outset. The Rimutaka Incline was an integral part of New Zealand's rail system from 1878 to 1955, and the only commercially successful centre rail system in the world.

Battling the giddying climb and ferocious winds the railway builders constructed a serpentine grade that became one of the seven railway wonders of the world. The Rimutaka Incline was a Kiwi icon. A new 8,798-metre-long tunnel made it redundant, and one of the most remarkable pieces of engineering on the New Zealand Rail system faded into antiquity.

When I first travelled from Wellington to Wairarapa the tunnel had been a going concern for 12 years. Not that the construction of the tunnel hadn't proved difficult, dangerous and time-consuming too. It took three years to bore a hole through the ranges.

I wonder what it might have been like travelling up the Rimutaka Incline. As the train bustles through the Rimutaka tunnel the mind wanders. Had I been born 10 years earlier I would technically have had the chance to experience the heavy staccato chuffing of the four or five Fell engines spaced strategically along the train. (No communication by corridor back then with the engines segmenting what would have been a longish train.)

It's hard to imagine what the whistling wind must have been like on exposed bends; three children were flung to their deaths once at a place named, aptly, Siberia, when a train was blown off the tracks. It's not for nothing they built wind barriers on strategic corners. Here in the

warmth of the train to Masterton all that seems long ago and almost in another dimension — a time and place where New Zealanders rejoiced in the climb away from what was then a landlocked Wellington, with the promise of exciting points north, like Napier in sunny Hawke's Bay, to visit even though smoke and soot had taken up residence in your clothes, and hair and bonnet were dishevelled by the devilish wind.

Wellingtonians spoke of travelling 'over the hill', conjuring up images of that magical yet arduous, smoky climb. Foreigners travelled to New Zealand just to take the ride to Summit on the Incline. My grandmother corresponded with a lady from Bournemouth for several years until her passing in 1968. They had met over a cup of tea at the Kaitoke refreshment rooms, clutching their hats and chatting about the way the surrounding scrubby trees were lying almost flat in the gale.

For those who have a good imagination and can picture the four- (or five-) engine passenger consists inching up the Rimutaka Incline, or simply for those who enjoy a good rail trail adventure over old embankments and bridges and through the tunnels of a once-famous railway, the Rimutaka Incline Walkway is highly recommended. It is an evocative way to experience what it might have been like all those years ago, with the Fell engines belching out grimy smoke and cinders. Not to mention the molten shards of metal off the brake shoes, which usually had to be changed after each gripping trip. The trail begins 10 km south of Featherston, the first stop beyond the tunnel, at the rail ghost town of Cross Creek. As yet there is no public transport to Cross Creek. Masterton-Wellington buses however, pass close to the Kaitoke end of the walkway and, bearing in mind that most visitors have committed themselves to a certain amount of walking, the short stroll to the walkway head can be considered a warm-up exercise.

The track passes through the 576-metre Summit tunnel where choking smoke, cinders and fearsomely hot surfaces made the job of engine drivers and firemen even more hazardous.

The centre rail of the Incline and the four horizontally-positioned mountain wheels beneath the Fell engines enabled the trains to gain adhesion. My grandmother said it was a bit like magic or 'something the menfolk know about'.

The menfolk also knew about the beer train that brought Saturday evening refreshments to the lonely Rimutaka rail settlement at Cross Creek at the base of the Incline. Wicked suggestions had it that railway men who had come to grief on other stretches of the New Zealand Rail system were banished to Cross Creek, the Siberia of the network in more ways than one. No road access, lousy winds, punishing work shifts. It was enough to make you hanker for the whistle of Saturday's beer train that brought in a few friendly ales to ease the privations.

A fireman from up north who had violated some regulation took to the Incline outpost like a duck to water. Or a fireman to beer. The Saturday beer train was common knowledge, but there were other services that saw the offloading of crates of something stronger and other concoctions from the capital. The banished fireman, whose original misdemeanour had been fired by alcohol,

OPPOSITE Heading for the hills. The Wairarapa train, made up of a motley carriage assortment, about to be engulfed by bush.

felt right at home in the desolate bush of the Incline.

Cross Creek folk covered for him. After all, his fellow townsfolk felt cut-off and shunned by authority as well. Many of them were recalcitrants too and the bonding was fierce. After five years of confabulation and conviviality the fireman was moved on again — to Hanmer Springs, the alcoholics' retreat. At least that's how my grandmother remembered it, through her sherry-haze.

That Cross Creek had a reputation as a wild-west railway town was confirmed by reports of inebriated gangers firing off a few rounds at the beer train as it nosed around the bend. Talk about biting the hand that fed, or lubricated, them. On other occasions unsanctioned trains climbed the Incline to the even more isolated Summit settlement to gather up partygoers wanting to kick up their heels back down in Cross Creek. After the 40-minute crawl up into the heavens (some saw it as hell) and surreptitious coasting back to Cross Creek, a certain amount of hell did break loose. The runaway line, a siding designed to stem the flow of trains stricken with brake failure, was always available if something more tangible than hell broke loose.

If you approach the walkway from the Wairarapa side it is possible to call at the Fell Engine Museum in Featherston, to view a rare beast: the only Fell engine remaining in the world. Somehow such a visit is an almost spiritual requirement before undertaking the walkway itself. The museum was established in 1984 by an organisation called the Friends of the Fell Society Inc. The nearby Heritage Museum, complete with artefacts from the World War II Featherston prisoner-of-war camp, is also worth a visit.

Beyond the tunnel, the 2007 train emerges into the Wairarapa. Following the swishing and crashing of the 8,798-metre bore, the peace and easy flow of the train on the other side signifies a different sort of experience. The glow of Lake Wairarapa and the charm of Featherston signals that this is no ordinary commuter train. Cell phones still chime, suits continue to alight, but away from the city this is the incarnation of an old-world provincial express train.

Families join the train. Grannies are helped aboard. Schedules are slightly behind. Sudden stops occur in the middle of nowhere. Fellow passengers remain friendly, if quiet, and the service even has an old-fashioned grumpy guard.

The Rimutakas recede behind us. Before too long the Tararuas glisten to the west. Out to the right, distant hills provide the eastern ramparts of the Wairarapa Valley. You imagine the ocean dashing itself on the lonely beaches, accessible only by no-exit roads, on the other side of those unknown hills.

The first stop in the Wairarapa is the antiquated, often quaint town of Featherston, now in many ways a dormitory town after serving time as a crucial rail settlement. The Wairarapa rail service feeds a road link, via Featherston, to the burgeoning wine town of Martinborough. The rail past meets the wine-growing present, and all the urbane sophistication that entails. Some of New Zealand's best red wines are produced in the Martinborough hinterland, which now boasts close to 20 wineries. The Wairarapa train services, particularly in the weekend, have become the transport mode of choice for many of the Wellington 'wine set' who get shuttled around the upmarket cafés, restaurants and wineries of Martinborough before crashing in swank guesthouses, cottages or the refurbished Martinborough Hotel.

Tranz Metro, which runs the trains, even offers a Wairarapa Gourmet Wine Escape package that includes train travel, shuttle services and accommodation.

Martinborough, formerly a small, forgotten, rural service town, has been transformed into a swept-up oasis on the back of the wine culture which, the wine buffs will insist, is not just about the famous Pinot Noir. It's also about Sauvignon Blanc, Cabernet Sauvignon and a very whimsical and piquant Riesling.

If the Martinborough phenomenon is a contemporary development, the Wairarapa in general is one of the oldest European-settled regions in New Zealand. The early arrival of the railway from Wellington assisted materially in opening up the region at a time when the completion of the main trunk section due north of the city was still problematic. The opening of the Rimutaka Incline in 1878 and the completion of the link to Masterton in 1880 meant the Wairarapa townships had a lifeline to the capital early in the piece.

First-time travellers are often surprised at the age of buildings and houses in Featherston, Carterton and Masterton. The incorrect assumption is often made that the Wairarapa was settled and developed late. Many of the old houses have been renovated in recent years, often by former Wellingtonians who commute, invariably by train, to the capital. As a consequence the towns have taken on a sparkling new aspect, one that probably would

not have emerged but for the continued availability of a regular train service.

Greytown, a settlement with an unusual rail history, is regarded as perhaps the most interesting of the Wairarapa towns. It was established as long ago as 1853 and through restoration and a sense of reinvention has retained a Victorian ambience.

The threat of flooding led to the railway bypassing Greytown yet at one time, in the late 1800s, it was the principal Wairarapa settlement. Its influence was significant and consequently a branch line was built from the junction at Woodside across the flood-prone five kilometres to the town.

The inauguration of the new branch was not auspicious. It rained incessantly on opening day in 1880, nobody rode the new service, there was no promotion, and little in the way of ceremony and joviality, factors normally associated with line openings at the time. Greytown publicans and shopkeepers were disappointed there was no influx of tourists.

The Greytown branch did not thrive, though in the early 1950s five trains a day still operated down the short spur. The standard train was the popular 'goods with car attached', only the car was usually devoid of passengers. Sheep and pigs as 'goods' were more heavily represented. In 1952 the number of trains was reduced to two a day when it became apparent that the Greytown branch was the poorest performing line in New Zealand.

Beyond Featherston the line carrying the 2007 service abandons State Highway 2, and curves in the lee of the Tararua foothills, through Woodside and Matarawa, to

Drifting along the Wairarapa Plains, a long way and far cry from the corporate canyons of downtown Wellington.

Carterton. In winter snow coats the Tararuas and the Wairarapa wind scythes through the valley, but there is a compensating country warmth among the locals. Woodside, the former junction for the short, ill-fated Greytown branch line and Matarawa, a small rural service settlement, see a smattering of passenger inter-change.

Carterton is more substantial and has become home to increasing numbers of Wellingtonians who continue to renovate formerly forgotten villas in the contemporary Wairarapa manner. Carterton is also well known as the small town where Georgina Beyer, New Zealand's first transsexual mayor, and later the world's first transgender member of Parliament, came to power.

Beyond Carterton State Highway 2 accompanies the

line again as it heads for the Wairarapa 'capital', Masterton.

Masterton Station harks back to the way New Zealand stations used to be. Admittedly there are no refreshment rooms as such, with guard rails, lino floor and great, battered tea pots waiting to replenish the travel-weary. But there is a café within the station complex. You can sit here, between trains, as your pie and coffee are brought to your table, and watch the diesel engine on the turntable out in the rail yard. Masterton Station, between trains, becomes an old-fashioned rail community. Several passengers have travelled the line simply to enjoy the rail experience, endure the archetypal grumpy guard, catch brunch within the confines of the station, and to gaze out on the railway yard and perhaps contemplate what we've lost in other parts of the country.

A friendly old man begins talking about the railcar days on this line. I figure we have something in common. I too travelled on the old Fiat railcar all the way from Wellington to Gisborne back in the 1960s. When the old guy rattles off some of the names allocated to the railcars — Mamari, Maahunui and Arai-Te-Uru — I realise he is casting back to an earlier period again, the era of the Wairarapa railcars, the 'tin hares', ushered in back in 1936 because of their comparative speed over the Rimutaka Incline.

'Those tin hares had their own personality, you know. They named them after Maori canoes. Give something a name and it becomes almost human, I reckon.'

The old guy was only ten when the railcars were unleashed. His recall is sharp. He can also remember when a Ford touring car on two sets of rail wheels was tested as a rail inspection car. It flinched a bit when the time came to mount the Rimutaka Incline. The driver was comfortable enough but the assistant ended up sitting on the bonnet nursing a bucket of water to cool the engine.

Such revelations suit the setting. If someone claims, as it is easy to do these days, that New Zealand no longer has a traditional rail environment, all they need to do is come to Masterton on a do-nothing Tuesday, set down at the station as the return service to Wellington is assembling and soak up the atmosphere.

Other travellers, regulars obviously, head for home. Those who caught the train at Carterton, twenty minutes back down the line, or at the Masterton suburban stations of Solway and Renall Street, head into town — Masterton — to do business, shop or whatever else suburban Mastertonians do. Another contingent, including those who have factored a train ride into their travels up through the Wairarapa, set out to explore Masterton and environs, including the Tararua Forest Park, before heading further north.

Back at the station the Masterton to Wellington train is ready to depart. Admittedly there are suits on any service, corporates in animated dialogue on cell phones but there are also ordinary travellers. Mothers with broods, lone bewhiskered blokes, a folksinger with guitar case at Matarawa, bare-midriffed teenage girls and large friendly Maori guys. This continues to seem like the reincarnation of your basic New Zealand Rail inter-city passenger express. As such, this train is a jewel — a reminder of what train travel could be in New Zealand; a glimpse, with its almost full carriages, at where New Zealand rail services will probably end up, thanks to road congestion,

Masterton rail yards. A surprisingly busy railway environment.

Further down the track at Woodside a mother attempts to find a place on the train for her teenaged daughter — without a ticket.

'It's not company policy to allow un-ticketed persons on to this train,' the guard yells from the carriage steps. 'This service is not a school bus.'

On the return journey the rural splendour of the Wairarapa Valley has been heightened by the clearing sky which sharpens the horizons off to the east. Beyond Featherston the road through Lake Ferry to Cape Palliser winds away beside Lake Wairarapa, a lake so expansive that first-time Kiwi travellers marvel at its size and want to know why such a watery gem has remained hidden from them for so long. Of course they won't know about the maritime splendour further south, where Lake Onoke drains into Palliser Bay on Cook Strait and all horizons, except the towering serrated peaks of the southern Rimutakas, are dominated by water.

Beyond Featherston the train veers due west above Pigeon Bush and returns to the black portals of the Rimutaka Tunnel and all that history above you. Beyond, Maymorn, Upper Hutt, Waterloo interchange and Petone pass by before the blue waters of Wellington Harbour presage our arrival at Wellington at midday, precisely. Or perhaps two minutes past.

For commuters the journey must make for a relaxing and contemplative means of getting to and from work. Pure workday blues therapy. For interlopers, tourists and casual travellers it is a pleasantly surprising and unsung diversion.

petrol prices and international environment imperatives, whether we like it or not.

The guard takes my ticket and seems to revel in the fact that the guard on the outward journey from Wellington has seen fit to punch the month of March, not April. He gives me a spiky stare, then drools over the gaffe.

'They've punched the wrong month, mate,' he whines through clenched teeth. 'They've got the right day, wrong month,' he emphasises.

The guard glares down for such a long time I suggest that perhaps I should leave his train. Whereupon he unleashes an unsettling spiel about how passengers have become the victims of administrative incompetence, although in my case, I could have taken greater responsibility for ensuring that my outward ticket was punched appropriately.

⑧ THE SCENIC SUBURBAN

WELLINGTON
TO JOHNSONVILLE

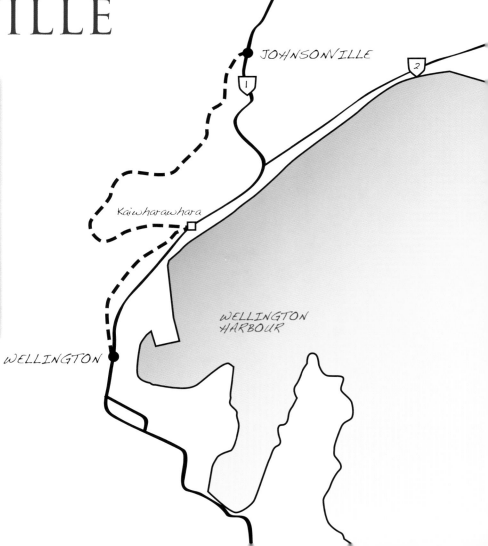

JOHNSONVILLE

Kaiwharawhara

WELLINGTON HARBOUR

WELLINGTON

T he most memorable suburban train ride in New Zealand is the 10.5–km service that connects Wellington central with the hill suburb of Johnsonville. In some ways it is an afterthought, a surviving remnant of the original main trunk route out of Wellington that was superseded by the Tawa Deviation and its two long tunnels, back in 1937.

The sense of history is profound as the electric unit pulls away from Platform 1, Wellington Station, Bunny Street. This is the way rail travellers used to depart the city in the days when the main trunk line began its climb through the Wellington hills a kilometre or two beyond the station yards. Before 1937 what now survives as the Johnsonville branch represented the first challenging section for all northbound passenger trains. The old expresses and limiteds to Auckland saw steam engines straining up the grade, over the highway bridge into the bushclad hills. Suburban trains to Paekakariki, and provincial services to Palmerston North, Napier and New Plymouth, were also obliged to leave the city along the serpentine stretch of line that demanded a slow struggle through scrub-fringed suburbs. Houses clung to hillsides. Random roads radiated out where the rugged terrain would allow, and train stations perched on upraised slivers or bush clearings.

After the Johnsonville train heads towards the hills just south of Kaiwharawhara to begin tracing the past, the line angles through the Ngaio Gorge. Most commuters don't dally over the history of the line. This is simply a quick way to get home to Crofton Downs, Ngaio, Awarua Street, Simla Crescent, Box Hill, Khandallah, Raroa and Johnsonville. Their glum expressions seem strangely disrespectful of the construction difficulties encountered by the work gangs who hacked this line through back in the early 1880s. Oblivious to the rail history associated with the line that for many years was the main route north out of Wellington, they complain, in 2007, about the ageing suburban train fleet consigned to the Johnsonville line. The narrow portals of the seven tunnels have stymied the upgrading of the electric units. They complain glumly about the poor upkeep of the carriages as the train screeches around the tight curves that carry it through the Ngaio Gorge, which looks for all the world

like the view from an ancient King Country bush railway. At least for half a kilometre.

This section of the line is vaguely disorientating, bearing in mind the presence of the New Zealand seat of government and the commercial bustle of Lambton Quay a few kilometres back down the track. But that is part of the line's appeal. It also has an heroic aspect. As a suburban route in danger of being closed down, it was saved in 1931 by heated public opposition to the government of the day's endeavours to either curtail services or offer the link to the Wellington City Corporation as an extension of their tramways system.

In 1938, a year after the opening of the Tawa Deviation and a more efficacious route north, the Johnsonville line was not only retained, but subjected to the first suburban electrification of a commuter route serving the capital.

Despite the good fight of earlier generations, contemporary commuters still complain, although the service runs trains every half hour. After only 20-odd minutes of picturesque ducking and diving the end of the line — Johnsonville — is reached. Mind you, most services are well-patronised and you get the feeling that the threat of withdrawal of the train would meet the same show of resistance that greeted the 1931 proposal.

To casual travellers the line is very much a boutique operation: the sort of scenic tourist route current entrepreneurs would bust a gut to develop. The train stops at eight quaint, well-maintained stations squeezed in between bush, hill and gorge, and the old snaking line.

Several parks and reserves are located along the line, within easy walking distance. Khandallah Park features scenic native bush three minutes' walk from Khandallah Station. The northern end of the Northern Walkway, a 16-km track, is accessible from near Raroa station. Regenerating native forest in Ngaio Gorge (Trelissick Park) and outstanding views across the city from the lookout on Mount Kaukau are highlights of the walkway. And simply walking the streets of the northern suburbs, between trains and intermediate stops (knowing you won't have to wait long for the next train), has its own appeal.

The train to Johnsonville leaves the harbour so early in its course that first-time travellers question their concept of time. They are used to such a sharp left turn occurring further along the harbour rim, where the main trunk heads towards the Tawa Deviation north of Kaiwharawhara. But this is the old main trunk route, one that served escapees from Wellington central for over 50 years.

Echoes of the old line reverberate as we jerk towards the hills, climbing exponentially. You can, if you try, almost hear the chuffing of an AB steam engine at the head of a swaying express as it struggles up the grade, and the clacking of knitting needles as grandmothers settle in for a long ride and young mothers make preparations to settle squawking infants, as normally reticent Kiwis of an earlier age speak volubly about their time in the capital.

How many New Zealand spurs like this one have been ripped up and disregarded, denying later generations a link with our rail past? Even this line, which used to run beyond Johnsonville, across the elaborate Belmont Viaduct, before coalescing with the current trunk at Tawa, is a truncated remnant.

OPPOSITE Electric traction through dramatic bush-fringed hills and still commuters complain.

At Crofton Downs schoolkids in wet uniforms invade the train, chattering and clattering, every second word a four-letter expletive. Most of the schools they go to are named Saint-something. The line climbs to its maximum height of 152 metres at Mount Misery (in honour of the glum commuters?) before levelling out at Johnsonville, the railhead, 142 metres above Wellington harbour.

Later in the day, with an hour to kill, I take another ride on the Johnsonville branch, like a kid on a roller coaster. The short line is so alluring and accessible. This time, on the way back, the usual clientele of black-uniformed office workers is complemented by bizarre alternatives: a quintet of downy-faced nuns cloaked in white habits with 'Go NZ' logos emblazoned from shoulder to shoulder; young women with bright yellow curly wigs and revealing Marlene Dietrich stocking suspenders; and another team of young men dressed in bright pink and burnt orange rugby jerseys, with eyewateringly luminescent green shorts extending almost to their clunking, long-studded rugby boots.

The Rugby Sevens tournament at Westpac Stadium (the 'Caketin') is about to be played out. Sartorial excess has become part of the on-field extravaganza for spectators and getting to the game — or games — in the Wellington manner means jumping on the regular train services that deposit fans virtually at the stadium door.

'I told Mr Prendergast I was going to the library to find some books on the metabolism of frogs,' one downy-faced nun said to another.

'He'll know you're wagging, Jason,' was the reply. 'The rugby's being televised.'

As the Johnsonville train creaks through the last tunnel on its downhill slalom and sweeps out over the highway bridge, it is a toss-up between taking in the expansive views of the harbour and the docks or staying focused on the bizarre entourage in our carriage, who have made the most interesting suburban train ride in New Zealand even more interesting. It's a change, albeit temporary, from the glum, grey-suited commuters who regard catching the service as humdrum as putting the rubbish out for collection.

The old English Electric rolling stock of the Johnsonville train sits stoically back at Platform 1. With its recent two-tone blue Tranz Metro makeover, it doesn't look a day over 50. But it is. The old units were let loose between 1948 and 1954 and as well as their facelift they are also being refurbished. Some probably already have been but no one seems to have noticed.

The Johnsonville train, the scenic suburban, is full of surprises. How many tourists and first-time travellers even know of its existence, and its clientele ranging from grim commuters to excited school kids? And at least once a year you get to see boys dressed as nuns and young women in suspenders as the train climbs and descends through bush fringes like an old central North Island stopping service. Only the glimpses of hillside suburbs through the clearings give it away.

Along with the short Melling surburban line at the mouth of the Hutt Valley, the Johnsonville route shares the distinction of being New Zealand's only line given over solely to passenger traffic. The passengers themselves should bear that exclusivity in mind.

⑨ THE HEINEKEN SPECIAL: THE CAPITAL CONNECTION

WELLINGTON TO PALMERSTON NORTH

M y final jaunt on the suburban trains of Wellington and its hinterland involves catching the Capital Connection, a specialised commuter service that leaves Wellington at 5.17 pm, after the average working day, and heads for Palmerston North in the Manawatu.

It runs only once a day so to experience the train's ambience it is necessary to stop over in Palmerston for the night before catching the next morning's service returning to the capital at 6.20 am.

Someone once said it's possible to judge a city's level of sophistication by the quality of its commuter train service. As you wait at Platform 8 for the 5.17 departure deadline, as the high heels stop clacking along the platform and murmuring, relaxed corporate-uniformed regulars settle into their spacious carriage enclosures, it is possible to sense the validity of the statement.

The Capital Connection is New Zealand's most sophisticated suburban commuter train. Whether that means Wellington is New Zealand's most sophisticated city remains debatable, but the smooth-riding train is certainly a tick in its box. Before you are completely aware of the swank surroundings, the train has moved beyond the Wellington yards and is angling around the harbour.

The very carriages of the Capital Connection are different. More distinguished and with an illusion of space created by their rectangular shape as opposed to the tubular aspect of typical Kiwi carriages. Then again, it's not an illusion — there is more space. The carriages are ex-British Rail stock and were purchased to introduce the travelling public of Wellington to the notion of one of the best commuter services in the world.

The train is air-conditioned, the toilets far more roomy. There is even a disabled person's toilet at the end of the café car. The buffet in the café car serves a wider range of goodies than other New Zealand train buffets. Chardonnay and Heineken do a roaring trade.

Passage to the buffet is aided by the side-winding pneumatic doors which make progress from carriage to carriage less demanding than the typical New Zealand situation where returning to your seat after visiting the buffet involves an act of some dexterity, juggling hot microwaved food and gushing cans of drink while grappling with stubborn door handles and straddling swaying intercarriage passageways.

The passengers, settling down with their drinks, are in

a position to enjoy the Kapiti Coast as the train emerges from the Tawa Deviation tunnels and rockets through all stations towards its first stop at Paraparaumu. The new technology is having a field day. Cell phones trill, executives plug into laptop sockets to check the markets, one spike-haired corporate is trimming his designer stubble with an electric razor. I-pods go on as Chardonnay seconds are eased down the wide aisle.

The late summer sun is going down over the Kapiti Coast, shafting light into the carriage, casting the dark-uniformed corporate army into deep shadow. On a fine day, like today, the Capital Connection appeals as a wonderful way to get home from work, an enchanted highlight. The train edges around one of the most scenic stretches of the main trunk, beyond Pukerua Bay, hugging the cliff above the tumbling Tasman.

With the wine and waning sun, the boisterous laughter and bonhomie, this could easily be a southern European service — along the Adriatic perhaps, on a stopping service to Dubrovnic. Off to the north, Kapiti Island encroaches on the horizon. Directly below on State Highway 1 juggernaut trucks clog an already blocked artery. Trapped car commuters thumb their steering wheels. Occasionally they glance up at the train as it coasts quietly beyond their point of desperation.

The Capital Connection doesn't even stop at time-honoured Paekakariki where simply everything along this line used to stop. It just ghosts past the road congestion and clustered conventional commuter passengers massing on the platform. This is a privileged commuter service and it's easy to begin imagining similar services in other New Zealand cities. Auckland to Helensville along the western line, with stops at Henderson and Waitakere; Christchurch to Lyttleton — or Rangiora; Dunedin to Port Chalmers.

At Paraparaumu the train finally makes its first stop. Many passengers alight here, creating a shadowy cloud on the platform as the sun dips, before heading for the car park. The stops are more frequent beyond the Wellington conurbation as the train heads inland through the Horowhenua towns of Waikanae, Otaki, Levin and Shannon. The sea is long forgotten now; the Tararua Ranges and Tararua Forest Park loom to the east. The train seems almost empty although a quartet of young men and women with dark glasses on their heads are chortling away at the head of the carriage. An attendant at the buffet is throwing Heineken cans and bottles into a rubbish receptacle that could conceivably be moved closer to his field of operation. He seems to be enjoying the chance to make a noise and test his aim.

'This train's a piece of cake after Paraparaumu,' he reckons. 'Prior to that you get a lot of corporate wannabes who treat you like shit.'

As darkness descends over the Manawatu plains the Capital Connection, so empty now of passengers you get the feeling that even the driver got off at Paraparaumu, swings through Linton, with its prison and military camp, and Longburn, which used to boast a major freezing works and a rail connection to Foxton. Suddenly we are in less privileged, not so corporate territory. With a brief lunge and a screech the train pulls into Palmerston North.

The Capital Connection seems like a hell of a way to get home from work. Compared to my grubby mid-60s

Corporate commuters contemplate their working day.

The main trunk corridor, stamping ground of the Capital Connection, shares a sliver of land with State Highway 1 along the Kapiti Coast.

commute from the old Beach Road, Auckland station to Mt Eden, it takes on aspects of the Orient Express. Set against road rage at the Queen City's spaghetti junction, gridlock at Grafton or Greenlane, the resulting burnt dinners at Balmoral or Birkenhead, or the forlorn looks from motorists at lovely Pukerua Bay back down the Capital Connection line, it looks eminently practical.

The Capital Connection is exactly what I haven't been expecting. This is a commuter train of the future as opposed to the Wairarapa and Johnsonville services which smack of the past. Admittedly long-lauded for its luxury by New Zealand standards, it needs to be experienced to truly appreciate its ambience. The return journey in the morning is just as absorbing, if a little less exultant, given that most travellers are confronting a day's work in the capital.

It's sobering to learn that the Capital Connection concept was introduced as long ago as 1991, and is New Zealand's longest commuter train route (140 km). The fact it's been running for 16 years makes the tardiness of other New Zealand cities in developing suburban services, sophisticated or otherwise, seem almost perverse. Even back in 1991 the Capital Connection enjoyed prestigious rolling stock by local standards. Surplus carriages from the old Northerner and Southerner main line circuits lifted the train out of the category of basic suburban commuter services. Sheepskin seat covers and an extra carriage were soon added when the positive public reaction to the new train was converted into a 10 percent increase in patronage.

Unlike many suburban trains the Capital Connection, from the outset, was classified commercial. It had to pay its own way and was not subsidised. The loyalty of passengers was rewarded when the upgraded British carriages, longer, wider and stronger, were first introduced in 1999.

More tourists too are using the comfortable train as a means of travelling north. The Overlander leaves Wellington at a challenging 7.25 am, requiring an early rise. The Capital Connection, towards the end of the day, not only boasts a more civilised departure time but, at the right time of year, uncovers scenic highlights not always available from the windows of the Overlander. It is also a relaxing way of accessing the beach resorts around Paraparaumu and Waikanae and the other tourist attractions in the area.

After a taste of the concentrated and efficient commuter services on the Hutt Valley and Melling lines (and the main trunk as far as Paraparaumu), the tasty aperitif of the Johnsonville branch and the sumptuous delight of the Wairarapa train, the Capital Connection provides a swank smorgasbord. Two or three days devoted to such travels whet the appetite for the Overlander Express.

But first, a diversion of quite a different kind.

⑩ A TRAIN RUNS THROUGH IT: THE ART DECO EXPRESS

PAEKAKARIKI TO NAPIER

I t's one of life's ironies that in Napier on the east coast of New Zealand's North Island, it took a catastrophe to produce something wonderful. In 1931 a devastating earthquake caused serious loss of life and the destruction of much of the town. From the ashes and rubble a new city emerged, built in the architectural style of the day. Over the years the distinctive Napier cityscape has acquired the tag 'art deco' and because of the concentration of such buildings in the Hawke's Bay city, locals were able to cash in on the appeal to tourists.

PREVIOUS PAGE Centre of attention. JA 1271, motive force of the Art Deco Express, attracts admirers and maintenance workers.

Something unique and with an unintended attraction for later generations emerged in the post-earthquake years, and these days the annual art deco weekend, which usually runs for four days in February, attracts thousands of visitors. A time-warp descends and first-time celebrants can be excused for thinking they have been spirited back to Napier in the 1930s.

In recent decades the wine industry has flourished in Napier and Hawke's Bay and many visitors to the art deco weekend are wine buffs, connoisseurs or simply enthusiastic tasters. While acknowledging the 1930s ambience of the event, they are prepared to concede that the free-flowing vintages are a more recent development. That doesn't stop them imbibing generously, appreciating that history often unfolds unevenly.

The steam-hauled passenger train that graces the art deco weekend is a recent development too, although it has an authentic 1930s feel to it. The art deco weekend is rendered more enticing because a train runs through it.

I don't know if the excursion train run by Steam Incorporated from Paekakariki to Napier is officially known as the Art Deco Express, but several passengers refer to it as such. I don't know how many years the steam-hauled train has been running on an annual basis to help celebrate Napier's Art Deco Weekend, but it certainly fired up in 2006 and 2007.

Paekakariki is the headquarters of Steam Incorporated, an excursion train operation run essentially by enthusiastic and remarkably professional volunteers and it is from Paekakariki that the Art Deco Express departs at 9.30 am.

Paekakariki Station now boasts a railway museum that provides good coffee and a jocular attendant who tells you all you need to know about the excursion train to Napier. Beyond the station the Steam Incorporated complex and angled approach line houses the Art Deco Express. JA 1271, an immaculately restored, New Zealand-built engine is discharging plumes of coal smoke through the spits of rain and blustery breeze to merge with the lowering clouds above the narrow shelf between the hills and the Tasman Sea.

Across the great divide of the Main Trunk, run by 'professionals', and the 'enthusiast' Steam Incorporated sidings, the nostalgic, distant singing sound of a steam engine at rest comes in on the breeze. That sound, like a thousand, synchronised cicadas, reminds me of days growing up in Te Kuiti on the Main Trunk line, and holds out great hope for a memorable journey.

Some excursionists have already ventured across the tracks to take their seats and generally check out the rolling stock and magnificent motive force. A cluster of art deco folk in flapper outfits and straw boaters and other period pieces wait on the station as JA 1271 gets up a powerful head of steam. Tranz Metro trains come and go. Commuters heading for the city in the electric units barely react to the excited clutch of excursionists in their 1930s clobber. After all, Wellington has become the 'dress-up' capital, thanks to events like the annual Rugby Sevens tournament — and the Art Deco Express.

'You have to expect a bit of soot in your straw boater,' a jovial travelling companion mentions, by way of introduction, as the train backs on to the main line and into the station. I suddenly feel underdressed in shirt, jeans and 60s suede shoes.

Dressed for the occasion. Art Deco folk sip tea and exchange pleasantries.

The train wastes no time once all the chortling passengers have clambered aboard. Despite the novelty factor, Steam Incorporated are utilising a busy, everyday rail corridor on the main trunk. Commuter trains are looming to the north and south.

With a shriek and a pounding of pistons the Art Deco Express pulls away, travelling along the Main Trunk for the first segment of the journey. I have been allocated a seat in Carriage B, a steel-clad 1930s car, which along with two further steel cars, five wooden carriages from the period 1908 to 1915, and a buffet car (which does an excellent bacon and egg muffin) that doubles as a souvenir booth and co-ordination centre for the train, make up a healthy total of nine carriages.

Our carriage is an exact replica of the cars I used to travel in on the Main Trunk expresses and limiteds. It carries the official number 1989, which is not the year of its construction, as one woman in a mauve ensemble and less than sensible shoes maintains. It is very much a product of the 1930s.

First stop, Paraparaumu. A rising sense of excitement is evident as more dressed-up folk clamber aboard. Even now as JA 1271 hoots and hollers through the widening rural stretches and smaller towns, people are bidden. Schools and kindergartens empty out as kids run across playgrounds towards the smoking monster pulling strange red carriages full of waving, dressed-up grown ups with friendly faces.

From time to time Steam Incorporated staff, including those assisting with feeding the voracious JA beast its diet of coal, and generally watering the steam components, wander down the corridor, seeking their own food and water at the buffet. One staff member looks familiar. As the train pulls into Otaki the penny drops. 'Otaki' was the title of one of my favourite Kiwi rock 'n' roll songs from the early 70s. A band called the Fourmyula, better known for another award-winning song, 'Nature', put 'Otaki' into the charts at a time when New Zealand's cultural cringe might have counted against such a landmark release.

It wasn't the done thing to write songs with New Zealand placenames as titles back then, not if they were intended for serious chart consideration. You could call your song Taumarunui or Timaru or even Paekakariki if you wanted to, but that immediately consigned it to the annals of folk music and folklore, not the hit parade.

'Otaki', the song, reached number 15 on the local charts, to defy the cringe and the man who wrote it, the founding member of the Fourmyula, was heading for the buffet again. Wayne Mason, dressed in fireman's garb, fringed with soot, was the familiar figure. Wayne is as passionate about steam engines as he is about music. These days he plays in his own band, Wayne Mason and The Fallen Angels, and is still writing and recording original songs. A new CD, 'Sense Got Out', was released in March 2008.

As the train pulls out of Otaki with the hammering pistons providing an aural back beat, the funky rhythms and melody of Wayne Mason's 'Otaki' reverberate in my head. Next stop Levin. At the Horowhenua town more cackling and jostling ladies in flapper gear and fascinators take their places in the wooden carriages. Palmerston North, before you know it. Here JA 1271 takes on water and more passengers.

Beyond Palmerston the onboard PA announcer highlights the point where the connection to the Hawke's Bay arcs away towards the east. The Main Trunk, complete with overhead wires, angles to the north. I haven't been on this stretch of track since the railcar days of the 1960s. Back then the very concept of a wind farm might have been seen as a cosmic happening, or perhaps the sort of conceptual art Yoko Ono might favour. Now, in the 21st century, a more mundane wind farm that generates electricity looms into view on the Tararua foothills. Giant windmills rotate like somersaulting Don Quixotes who've done their tilting.

The narrow cleft of the Manawatu Gorge begins with two tunnels and soon the train is winding through one of New Zealand's more remarkable communication routes. Across the river State Highway 3 straddles the steep gorge, with much of the road bed being supported and supplemented by concrete piles. Along the gorge diversion, cars are parked on narrow ledges and their occupants wave and gawp and aim their cameras.

The scars from flooding and landslides attest to the difficulty of maintaining a roadway through the divide between the Ruahine and Tararua Ranges. The railway line has its own problems, particularly with a steam-hauled train. We are advised to close all windows and doors while threading the early, longer tunnels and when the three short bores at the eastern end are encountered, we learn that these are due to be converted into cuttings to accommodate the larger container wagons scheduled to run on the Hawke's Bay line.

Beyond Woodville, the junction town for the Hawke's Bay and Wairarapa lines, the spectacular hill country brings back memories. The first time I travelled on the line it was a showery mid-week day when, out of the blue, my employer granted annual leave that had to be taken immediately or forfeited. By a happy coincidence it had become apparent, thanks to an advertisement on the walls of Te Kuiti Station, that passenger travel around provincial New Zealand was still possible, despite the withdrawal of several services. At a time when the big OE beckoned, the notion of travelling by railcar from

The 'Art Deco Express', expertly run by Steam Incorporated, waits at Palmerston North. Bill Anthony, excursion manager, strikes a successful pose.

Palmerston North to Napier, and even further north-east to Gisborne, appealed as a holding pattern until the big jet headed out for London or LA.

As the sun emerged in 1967 the yellowing hills of Hawke's Bay were a sight of such surprising beauty they put my overseas travel plans into temporary recess. Forty years later the hills of Hawke's Bay are no less striking. From the more rugged reaches between Woodville and Dannevirke to the rolling landscapes beyond, it's still distinctively different from the green and grey vistas of home. Layered hills angle to the eastern horizon. Some seemed sculpted, others scalloped. Some look like camel humps and shark fins as the sun casts shadows in some places and highlights the bright yellows and muted browns and greens in others.

Villages like Papatawa, and lonely farm bungalows and villas located on the domed hills and plateaux, remind the traveller of the human component. A woman in a wheelchair on the front verandah waves frantically while kids at a tiny country school are already assembled at the schoolyard fence to ogle at the train. At Oringi the complex that serves as the collection point for milk from the growing number of dairy farms, flits past. Milk trains, a relatively new development, run from Oringi to the massive dairy factory at Whareroa near Hawera on the Taranaki line.

By now Bill Anthony, the excursion manager of the Art Deco Express, has made himself known to travellers. He is a jovial fount of knowledge about Steam Incorporated and is justifiably proud of its operation. It's a slick service, well patronised, and reflects the desire of travellers and rail fans to touch base with trains heading out over lines far removed from the main rail routes.

A sense of camaraderie among the passengers has developed in the time it's taken to get from Palmerston North to Dannevirke, the first fully-fledged town along the Hawke's Bay line. After the long haul from Woodville to Dannevirke, one Englishman's thirst is apparent. It would be most appropriate, he reckons, if there were a pub within a stiff walk of the station where the train is due to stop for forty minutes for servicing — to wit, more water and coal.

Beyond the cheering, waving gaggles of locals on the platform, the Merrylees Hotel is directly opposite the station and we waste no time in finding the public bar. The Englishman and I simply follow the woman in the pink and green ensemble who announces her determination to track down a decent Hawke's Bay chardonnay. The locals in the bar are amused at the contrast between their truck driver's garb, occasional bush singlet, work boots and jandals, and the extravagantly coiffured ladies. Not to mention blokes in straw boaters, striped waistcoats and Great Gatsby white strides, who slop beer with the best of them. The T-shirted bar ladies are only too delighted to serve the house chardonnay to the art deco Wellington women in their mauve outfits, teetering high heels and roaring twenties rouge.

As the hard-working train staff work overtime, the Englishman and I feel distinctly privileged as we sip our beer and watch the people of Dannevirke marvelling at the sight of a passenger train and, even better, a real live steam engine. The fact that many of the passengers look like something out of *The Girlfriend* adds to the allure.

After a counting of heads, the train storms away from Dannevirke station, past the Dannevirke club where patrons lean against the fence, waving with one hand and cupping their handles in the other. Following the watering of the passengers the mood on board is even more jovial as the line returns to the rural recesses. Free-range photographers are sighted on riverbanks, halfway up hillsides where they straddle the grade like sheep, or set themselves up on overhead pedestrian bridges.

We are in viaduct country now and Ormondville presents another phalanx of raucous supporters as the train glides past the local hotel and another lineup of ordinary country blokes variously waving and drinking beer toasts to the Art Deco Express. This is short-back-and-sides country, although one young guy is sporting a longer, purple and black dye job to provide contrast.

The train doesn't stop at Ormondville Station, despite its growing reputation as a converted bed and breakfast accommodation option. It can house up to eight guests and has been so well refurbished that it recently won an award of some note. Then we are on the curving Ormondville viaduct, one of the highlights of the journey, an impressive 280 metres long and 39 metres high.

The line passes through Takapau and enters a straight stretch of track that heads due east, skirting Lake Hatuma before reaching Waipukurau, a hilly portion of which has been looming for some distance. The really lonely reaches are behind us now, the layered hills wavering in the fading late afternoon sunlight and receding to the east.

At Waipukurau a large group of kids board the train. Their excitement is intense on the short haul to Otane, where their ride ends. Outside the good folk of Otane are variously dumbfounded, awestruck or overjoyed, depending on age. For some a steam-hauled passenger train through here stirs fond memories of less challenging times when train travel provided a safer option than the roads do now. The five white crosses on the Otane station approach road are one of the few sobering aspects of this journey.

For some a steam-hauled passenger train takes them back to the days when small boys attempted to outpace the likes of JA 1271 and its nine red carriages on bikes, just as they do today. As we sprint away, in an attempt to make up an inconsequential sliver of lost time, today's little Johnnies and Jasons find themselves outpuffed and chuffed before they coast to a stop and in a more contemporary gesture pull out cell phones to photograph the retreating train.

From here to the end of our journey at Napier everything accelerates. An almost surreal light suffuses the hypnotic yellow hills of wine country as more and more people emerge from houses, pubs, shops, packing sheds, garages and factories to acknowledge the passing of a phenomenon that no longer features in their lives, if it ever did. Everyone waves. Even sheepish men who don't normally wave at inanimate objects. But then perhaps they are waving to us — especially the pretty, dolled-up ladies who wave back like royalty.

Kids run towards the smoking monster, now shrieking and clattering across the flats of the Heretaunga Plains. The pied-piper magnetism of JA 1271 is evident in the joyous faces of kids of all ages. A woman rushes from her house towards the train at Pakipaki, wrapped in a bath towel. One hand secures her dignity while the other waves fervently. A young girl on a bike smiles spontaneously. You can see the sense of wonder in her eyes. Even a carload of black-clad bogans in a lowered Mazda pull over, leap out and punch the air. I don't see a single derisory gesture as the Art Deco Express hammers home its advantage.

Deep green fields of squash and pumpkins alternate with jungles of apple orchards, their trees stooping with fruit ready for picking. Have we entered the Garden of Eden? Is this train bound for glory?

At Hastings, evidence of art deco buildings engenders

Women passengers in their finery on Dannevirke station.

excitement among the passengers, some of whom are by their own admission 'quite relaxed', thanks to the shots of local chardonnay acquired by the bottle back at the Dannevirke pub. The woman from Invercargill continues waving from the window long after the rest of us find something else to do with our hands. It's what they do down south — wave at trains. Not unlike the people of Hawke's Bay, many of whom have parked beside State Highway 2 to welcome the train into Napier. The sea suddenly appears. The small dark blue car, and its driver/photographer who has shadowed us all the way from Dannevirke, are now silhouetted against the bright blue of the Pacific as the line straightens along the coast, through Awatoto and past the Norfolk pine-fringed attractions of Marine Parade.

Napier city is upon us in a rush. City dwellers are just as effusive as the train pulls out of its surge and eases into the station, packed with sight-seers and wellwishers. If we were all heroes returning from war, it would make more sense. But then you realise that apart from friends and family welcoming passengers off the train, it is the steam engine that captures the collective imagination.

JA 1271 is a sleek machine. The JA was always my favourite steam engine. The Ks and KAs were more bulbous and utilitarian, like rugby forwards. The JAs and their sister ships, the Js, were more your fleet-footed wing three-quarters and ghosting inside backs.

In many ways the Art Deco Express is a ladies' train. Sure, the men who have dressed for the occasion are dapper enough, but the women's outfits are often walking works of art, fit to kick off the art deco weekend in fine style as they cluster on the platform. Even JA 1271 has feminine lines, unlike the bulky Ks and KAs with their solid, square tenders. JA 1271 is tapered in all the right places with a rounded tender bringing up the rear. Her whistle shrills musically, if insistently, unlike the deeper peel of the Ks and KAs, which was more like a sergeant-major's bark sounding across the rugged terrain of the Main Trunk's central North Island stamping ground.

Steam Incorporated's JA sits sizzling at Napier Station as cameras click and flash and eyes boggle. It has a busy long weekend ahead of it, being scheduled to haul local excursions to Wairoa, Hastings, Otane and Holts Forest, before returning to Paekakariki with its distinctive red carriages in tow on Sunday afternoon.

Slightly disoriented by the events of the day, I take to the streets of Napier where the sense of expectation is tangible. Everyone is talking about the Art Deco Express. You reach the reasonable conclusion that if the government and Pharmac wanted to halve their Prozac bill they could do worse than schedule their own steam-hauled vintage trains to run through down-at-heel New Zealand. Steam engines, bright red carriages and passengers dressed in the fashion of our grandmothers' time certainly seem to elevate the mood.

It has been such a galvanising gallivant through Hawke's Bay that it reconfirms my belief that everyone should have the chance to ride on such a train. Better still, try the Art Deco Express itself. It's one of the best.

⑪ THE HOMING PIGEON: THE OVERLANDER

WELLINGTON TO TE KUITI

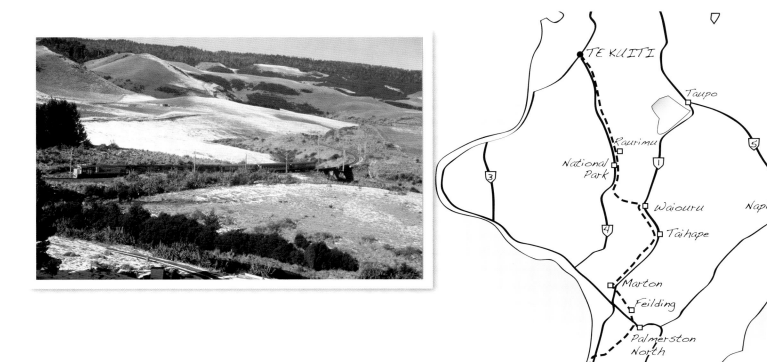

The Overlander route, between Wellington and Auckland and vice versa, covers many scenic options. The train edges along the rocky coastline of the Kapiti Coast, climbs to the central plateau and Tongariro National Park and descends through the rugged King Country to the verdant Waikato Plains. Along the way it negotiates one of the world's most dramatic and fervently-awaited railway spirals and catches up with the wide, slow-moving Waikato River on its way to the sea. As the day winds down, recollections return of the gaping white escarpments where the newer viaducts of the Rangitikei River Valley complement those of the old central North Island viaducts in isolated territory where settlements produce a sense of surprise.

PREVIOUS PAGE The Overlander in the North Island high country.

The central hamlets, villages and more developed towns often nestle in rugged valleys or rise defiantly on plateau or escarpment. The very existence of such lonely outposts is due to the groundbreaking railway line that not only opened up the central heartland of the North Island but, as the importance of the railway receded, also provided essential staging posts for travellers passing through by road. Often these former rail outposts now owe their survival to tourist operations that have seen everyday activities like sheep shearing sold to tourists as an attraction, simply because sheep shearing is a novelty to many. Similarly, the rugged, often unforgiving grandeur of the heartland recesses are now being accessed by walking tracks, highly prized by a new generation of travellers.

Cities developed along the route: Palmerston North, 144 kms north of Wellington, and Hamilton, a similar distance south of Auckland. Ironically, in 2007, electrification of the line extends between these two, often maligned, provincial cities. Maligned perhaps because of their landlocked status in an island country, where beside the sea is often seen as the only place to be.

From sea to sea. If one of New Zealand's claims to fame is its island status, with no community further than 200 kilometres from the ocean, the Overlander appears to lose points as it plunges into one of the most landlocked passages on the New Zealand rail system. Hence the train's name. It leaves the yawning harbour of Wellington by burrowing into the sturdy hills immediately to the north, through the double-tunnel complex of the Tawa Deviation. It seems of little consequence that the Overlander from Auckland plunges into a tunnel too — the short Glen Innes bore, the only one in the less upthrust Auckland hinterland, but it could be seen as similarly symbolic.

Te Kuiti in the King Country was where it all started for me. I can just about remember breaking curfew and toddling out of our clay compound up on the Te Kuiti hills all those years ago. I can almost recall my wilful sense of defiance as I wandered off at 5.30 am and four years of age, answering the call of the K engine as it drew the Wellington to Auckland Limited into our valley not long before the sun burst over the Rangitoto Hills. The Limited was one of the steadfast forerunners of the Overlander.

Now in 2007, I am heading home again. Wellington to Te Kuiti on the Overlander. The following day I will complete the journey from Te Kuiti to Auckland. Te Kuiti is not recorded as a major stop on the Overlander daily timetable. I could take umbrage but concede that Te Kuiti — and the railways — have lost ground since my display of defiance way back when. Not that Te Kuiti is my home

any more anyway. But I have managed to tee up digs with an old friend who still lives there.

At seven o'clock in the morning Wellington Station is relatively calm. The suburban stampede has yet to really kick in. Our train, the Overlander, is waiting at Platform 8, the lights going on in the carriages. It is due to depart at 7.25 am and twelve hours later, after the longest train ride in New Zealand (585 kilometres in fact), it is scheduled for a 7.20 pm arrival in Auckland. Te Kuiti is about two-thirds of the way up the track.

Wellington Station is the hub of a city system that is the busiest in New Zealand. Wellingtonians took to the trains in a way that suggested a different mindset from other New Zealand urban dwellers. It helps that all services funnel into the main station, which in turn opens out on to the corporate canyons that make up a compact CBD. While the compactness has been dictated by the towering hills surrounding the downtown area, which in turn has enhanced the practicality of train access, you also get the feeling that Wellingtonians over the years found their often conservative, sober needs well met by the steady suburban train service. Being the seat of government and the base for head offices, there were fewer of the maverick, private-enterprise outriders associated with Auckland and elsewhere.

Wellington Station soon hums with humanity. The wind whistles in the front entrance, welcoming commuters to their working day in the city. The eddies tug at a woman's hat as she sips tentatively at takeaway coffee. Mens' ties are whipped over their shoulders. An unseasonable cold snap has caught many out. Shirt sleeves and summer

tops are no match for the rising northerly and there is an added spring in the step of commuters, seeking the solace of office or corporate tower.

A homeless man rises from his bed on a bench near the ticket office, disturbed by the clustering, space-invading commuters who look stoically ahead, beyond the man's grubby sleeping bag and wild appearance. The northerly won't trouble him. He sports a layered look of Swanndri, bush shirt and blue Otago rugby jersey over fleecy trackpants and work socks. His lack of shoes could become a problem as showers sweep into the city on the back of the wind change, but then wet feet seem like the least of his problems.

I take my place on the Overlander and feel the old tingle of excitement. The tingle can be traced right back to boyhood. Perhaps it's a conditioned reflex, or something deeply pathological. If I was climbing aboard the 'Glory train' scheduled to take me to meet my maker, there would still be that tingle, I reckon. Anyway it doesn't last long. There are practical issues to attend to, like making sure no one has flogged your window seat. When you find that an attractive American woman has in fact flogged your window seat, you set about activating recently acquired assertiveness techniques and make your approach. Before you have a chance to make a fool of yourself you realise you are in the wrong carriage. At about the same time the American woman rises, exclaiming that she too is in the wrong carriage. I head aft and she forward. It's still early in the morning for many of us and it will take a couple of stiff coffees to stimulate accurate decision making.

With little fanfare the Overlander begins moving. No

engine whistle that I can hear, no PA announcement. Everyone is accounted for. No call for last-minute histrionics with latecomers sprinting into the wind. It's my contention that the rail experience in Wellington is enhanced by squally weather. Rural settings look desolate in the rain but the city and seascapes of the capital take on a wild beauty as the wind buffets and white caps jostle. You feel snug and a little smug inside the warm carriage as, outside, Wellingtonians brave the weather to get where they have to go.

One of the most memorable summertime experiences of the journey down the Overlander route from Auckland is emerging from the Tawa Deviation tunnels into the light and sweeping across the face of Wellington Harbour. After the dark, the broad expanse of glinting water and the sight of homes perched on precarious cliffs makes you want to turn around and do it again.

Going north, the drama is less intense. Indeed, if you are travelling in winter and given the Overlander's 7.25 am departure, the shift from the semi-gloom of the harbour to the total darkness of the long tunnels is barely discernible. Compensation for northbound travellers comes with the traverse of the Kapiti Coast. Southbounders may miss the scenic delights of the coast if they are travelling in the early evening darkness of winter.

The train disappears into the first of the two long tunnels of the Tawa Deviation, at which point the Overlander's internal life comes into focus. Most carriages are almost full. Many passengers are middle-aged tourists, husbands and wives mainly, although in this day and age that's just an assumption. In our carriage there are several younger tourists with backpacks and one or two family groups.

As the train comes up for air and crosses the Ngauranga Gorge bridge between the two tunnels, a hint of sunlight glints before we plunge back into the hole in the hill. At the head of the carriage a strangely familiar form is seen negotiating the doorway. His blue Otago rugby jersey is a bit of a giveaway. As the wild-looking man last seen rising from the station bench edges down the corridor, most passengers not already sharing a seat look pointedly and meaningfully out the window, although there's nothing to see but tunnel darkness and misshapen reflections. The man hovers near my seat — 12D — for several seconds before moving further back.

Beyond the Tawa Deviation tunnels the Overlander has right of way through the commuter stations between the city and the Kapiti Coast. The sun comes up as the train threads its way through Porirua city and out along Porirua Harbour towards Paremata and Mana. This harbour, a glistening jewel in the early morning, was once earmarked as the main sea-lane for the city of Wellington. Then an earthquake reduced its depth and pioneer aspirations turned south to Wellington Harbour where, despite natural wind funnels, deeper water beckoned.

Beyond Plimmerton and Pukerua Bay the Overlander's course — the Main Trunk line — reaches the open Tasman Sea coast.

The train is soon travelling along the Kapiti Coast as the sky clears and the misty shrouds are blown away. The coffee from the buffet goes down well as the prospect of better weather lifts the spirits and, one hopes, the cloud cover around Mt Ruapehu on the central plateau six hours away.

OPPOSITE Panoramic windows reflect the angling sun as the Overlander heads north.

The Overlander's course along the Kapiti Coast is one of New Zealand's most dramatic rail passages. The TranzCoastal's 100-km transit along the South Island's Pacific Coast is an awe-inspiring marine route, but the climb along the Kapiti Coast between Pukerua Bay and Paekakariki is dramatic in its own way because it features a precipitous passage above the ocean, through inevitable tunnels, with views overlooking a meagre highway where constipated city traffic edges by. The open ocean view is only interrupted by the southern reaches of Kapiti Island, one of New Zealand's most notable bird sanctuaries.

Birdlife that has become rare or extinct on the mainland thrives on the island. Tui, bellbirds, fantails, wood pigeons, kaka, weka and kakariki and a handful of the 200 takahe still in existence, can be sighted from the Trig, Wilkinson or North tracks that interlace the island.

The island also has a bloody past. It was in 1822 that Maori chief Te Rauparaha overwhelmed the original inhabitants and set up a base for his Ngati Toa people. Te Rauparaha is believed to be buried on Kapiti and the island has a spiritual dimension for the Maori people.

Despite its sanctuary status limited numbers of visitors may visit the island on day trips on the back of landing permits issued by the Department of Conservation. Launches connect the island with Paraparaumu Beach.

'This is us here,' an elderly Englishman announces to his wife and what appears to be their grandson. They must have got on at Porirua, although I'm not sure we stopped there. Either that or they've been searching for their seats since Wellington. The Englishman takes the aisle seat next to me. After jostling his carry-on luggage

under the seat he introduces himself as Reg Pike from Cornwall. He is an affable, quietly spoken man with a good sense of humour and the best interests of his family at heart. It's not long before he's unfurling provisions like ham, tomato and cheese, and handing snacks back to his wife and grandson in the seats behind us. Reg is from Dawlish on the coast of Cornwall and between mouthfuls of a very early lunch he gets to talking about his time working for British Rail. He never actually says what it was he did for British Rail, but I assume from the nature of the conversation that he was an engineer of sorts.

The Kapiti Coast is now sparkling, the cloud cover burned off. I offer Reg my window seat, which he politely declines.

The line hugs the hills as the train pulls into Paekakariki. This used to be the last refreshment stop, heading south, before the final stretch that took travellers into Wellington central. The trains were always set to stop at Paekakariki for this was also where the electric engines took over from the steam-driven. These days Paekakariki is the setting for the Steam Engine Museum and the steam engine excursion train operation, Steam Incorporated.

The line heads inland beyond iconic Paekakariki. Paraparaumu, a few kilometres further on, boasts a McDonalds Restaurant comprising a preserved Kerr Stuart steam loco and a madeover heritage carriage. Waikanae sees the Main Trunk heading north beside the lowering Tararua Ranges towards Horowhenua and the Manawatu, through market gardening and light-industrial centres like Otaki and Levin on the way to the major junction centre of Palmerston North. Tararua

Forest Park rises to the East. Shannon, with its splendidly restored station, takes the fancy of rail buffs.

Someone's done a job on the 'Palmerston North' signs along the platform, as we pull into 'Student City' about 9.30. Certain letters have been removed from 'Palmerston North', leaving interesting variations like 'Erston Orth', 'Palm Nort', 'Ston No' and 'Pal Nor'. A bit confusing perhaps for foreign travellers.

The Overlander stops for 15 minutes at Palmerston North and a good number of local passengers clamber aboard.

Palmerston North is often ignored by tourists despite its status as the thriving centre of the Manawatu Region and an education hub of significance. With the arrival of the railway in 1886, Palmerston burgeoned from a collection of crossroads buildings to one of the country's largest and most lively inland cities. The student presence enlivens the town and fine museums, galleries and libraries complement the array of bouncing bars and restaurants. Massey University, with its accent on agricultural research and more generalised academic delving, helps make Palmerston North distinctive.

Beyond Palmerston North, where the line used to run through the heart of town and where junction spurs serve Hawke's Bay and Wairarapa via the Manawatu Gorge (you can see the lines arcing off towards the east), the Main Trunk heads north beyond the suburbs, through Bunnythorpe and Feilding, across the Manawatu Plains to Marton Junction.

The Feilding District Steam Railway Society, based in the Feilding railyard, has developed a high profile thanks to the tractive effort of its restored WAB engine, which has been whistled up to haul the occasional Overlander through the heartland to Ohakune. JA 1250, from the northern base of Pukekohe, has also been roused from its slumber at the Glenbrook Vintage Railway to haul the southbound Overlander into the King Country on special days, as far as Te Kuiti, where a recently installed turntable re-aligns the elegant steam engine to pull the northbound service later in the day.

In steam days Marton was a lively centre. I last recall the Wanganui junction town in rather bizarre circumstances. Seven passengers and five assembled and remarkably well-behaved sheep stood motionless on the platform. Someone suggested this might be some sort of local tourist promotion, along the lines of Taihape's annual light-hearted gumboot throwing competition. Whoever hurls the gumboot furthest takes out the title. Was sheep-throwing about to become Marton's tourism salvation?

You can see lines branching away from Marton Junction too — the tracks to Taranaki, via Wanganui. Soon the Overlander feels the pull of the gradient as the line begins to climb towards the Rangitikei River escarpments where to the east, in the Mokai Patea Range, the last sighting of the huia bird was reputed to have been made.

The handsome huia was found only in New Zealand. Shiny black feathers, white-trimmed tails, bright orange wattles and a distinctive birdsong made them much sought after. The male and female had strikingly different beaks and the long curved appendage of the female was as prized as the feathers. Both Maori and European, as well as four-legged predators, contrived to render the mystical

Between Ohakune and Horopito the Hapuawhenua viaduct, a 'state of the art' structure completed in 1987 to replace the old steel version, provides passage for the Overlander.

its DC3 aircraft converted into a café, recedes as the Overlander heads north-east.

I happen to be leaning against the buffet car window as the Overlander begins its trek through the Rangitikei River country, a stretch marked by several massive concrete viaducts.

An extensive deviation was constructed through here in recent times, with the concrete viaducts being the significant feature. From my position hard up against the window I am afforded a yawning view of space as the train eases across the bridges. I come away with a better impression of how a bungy jumper might feel, about to dive from a great height.

The climb continues through Utiku before Taihape comes into view. Yet the Rangitikei River country remains embedded in the mind. From one of the viaducts you could see kayakers negotiating rapids, hundreds of feet below. After the pleasant rural scenes as the Manawatu Plains receded, the dramatic aerial route through and beyond Mangaweka has served to rouse the train's population. Cameras click, camcorders whir. American accents are thick in the air.

The Overlander curves westward through Taihape. On some road maps a reference to 'gumboot throwing' is directed at Taihape. It's a matter of a forsaken railway town reinventing itself. The annual gumboot throwing event has become as significant as the Wild Foods Festival in Hokitika, or the 'running of the sheep' through Te Kuiti, a fair stretch up the track. That Taihape no longer has a railway focus is confirmed as the Overlander, making up time, sweeps through the station adjacent to the main

birds — sacred (or tapu) to the Maori — extinct.

The Mangaweka region used to be cloistered by night for train travellers. Nowadays on the Overlander you see the line edging around white cliffs and roaring across viaducts, while the Rangitikei River, like a plaything, dawdles through the valleys far below. The township of Mangaweka, nestled near an escarpment edge, with

OPPOSITE Jewel in the scenic crown. Mount Ruapehu parades its glory to Overlander passengers.

street where SUVs and gumbooted locals act out cameos in a silent movie set against old, grimy buildings and railway houses that no longer accommodate railway workers.

The train staff, via the PA system, suggest that the climb up to Waiouru could be arduous. It's no big deal for passengers who have developed an affection for the Overlander and its pilgrimage through the centre of the North Island. It's no price at all to pay on a critical phase of the longest train ride in New Zealand.

For several circuitous kilometres the line disappears through the Hautapu River Valley, before emerging at Turangarere where State Highway 1 catches up. Hihitahi passes and soon the land turns subalpine as the central plateau reveals tussocky, windswept landscapes and mountain views at Waiouru, lonely base of New Zealand's largest army camp, a significant army museum and the highest station in New Zealand at 814 metres above sea level, before the line turns due west through Tangiwai, sad setting of New Zealand's worst rail disaster.

The Tangiwai disaster, in which 151 people lost their lives, was an inconceivable tragedy to occur in New Zealand in 1953. I can still recall the sad monotone of the National Radio announcer reading out the names of the victims as we sat down to Christmas dinner. The crater lake on Mount Ruapehu had burst, discharging an evil lahar that wiped out the rail bridge at Tangiwai 30 minutes before the Wellington to Auckland express arrived at the crossing point. We learned about lahars and sadness. I remember my grandmother sobbing through Christmas dinner after hearing the name of an old friend read out.

A memorial has been erected to honour the memory of the victims. Its location is pointed out via the onboard PA system, but even before that the train has gone eerily quiet. Kids have stopped running up the corridor, babies have settled. Grown-ups' conversations have petered out. We cross the weeping waters (the Maori meaning of Tangiwai) and even the throb of the engine seems muted.

Beyond Tangiwai the Overlander gathers pace across country through Karioi and past its large sawmill before easing into Ohakune.

Talk about reinvention. Ohakune, another old-world railway town, indeed a junction, for the brief spur to Raetihi used to branch off here, has become a ski town within easy distance of the Tongariro National Park. Mount Ruapehu and the Turoa skifields are located up the Ohakune Mountain Road. Tongariro National Park, off to the east, is the setting for three active volcanoes: Tongariro (1968 m), Ngauruhoe (2290 m) and Ruapehu (2796 m). There are no trains to Raetihi any more, but a cluster of ski chalets, tourist hotels and contemporary restaurants attest to Ohakune's altered status. Two kilometres to the west, central Ohakune has also adapted to changing times in which modern tourists see the Overlander simply as a means of getting to the skifields and vertiginous walking tracks.

Tongariro National Park is unique. It became New Zealand's first national park in 1887, when the chief of the Tuwharetoa tribe, aware that European land-grabbing would lead to the development (or desecration) of sacred Maori lands, gifted the vast expanse of mountain-studded territory to the developing nation. In return Tuwharetoa asked that the spectacular scenic wonderland not be settled or carved up. Whakapapa village was established,

OPPOSITE National Park, the crossing point. North and South-bound Overlanders pass in the lee of Mount Ruapehu.

The remarkable Raurimu Spiral. Two tunnels, three horseshoe curves, one complete circle and quite a bit of head spinning.

Circuit. And of course, many more come for the skiing.

Eventually, as the Overlander completes its long, slow climb from Taihape, through Waiouru and Ohakune up to the volcanic plateau, the train staff make ready to alight. Next stop is National Park where train crews swap over. The region known as the King Country begins beyond Ohakune. This is one of the more remote and desolate parts of New Zealand, acquiring its name when the Maori King Tawhiao and followers of the King movement retreated south after the Land Wars of the 1860s. Pakeha settlers and Maori had taken up arms against one another, and the rugged natural fortresses south of the Puniu River, near the Waikato town of Te Awamutu, became a Maori stronghold.

Construction of the main trunk railway line was delayed for many years. The King Country was too dangerous for rail construction gangs until the 1880s when peace was made with Maori and the line finally inched its way through the rugged hinterland.

The arrival of the railway opened up a region that was virtually the last major tract of territory in New Zealand to be subjected to European influence.

National Park, up on the central plateau, sees the two Overlander trains — northbound and southbound — meet at the modest station, lying in the lee of Mount Ruapehu.

Not so long ago, National Park station was a private residence. As preposterous as that notion might sound now — and to older generations for whom a rail network meant trains carrying people, stations serving trains — such aberrations did occur. Market forces decreed that many stations that weren't nailed down, and even some that

at the end of a purpose-built access road, and a grand hotel, the Chateau Tongariro, was constructed to serve the accommodation needs of holidaymakers. The park is located on the Taupo volcanic zone, and in 1996 train travellers were privileged to see a 12-km high plume of volcanic ash and dust blasting skyward as Ruapehu repeated the eruptive performance of the year before. That the three volcanic peaks of the park are still regarded as active adds to their allure.

Many tourists use the Overlander as a means of accessing two of New Zealand's most arresting tramps — the Tongariro Crossing and the Tongariro Northern were, went under the hammer. National Park Station was later converted into a café, which is how we find it today.

This is as close as the modern rail system comes to replicating the old refreshment stop days. Refreshment stops at Taihape, Ohakune and Taumarunui in those days acquainted passengers with the icy air outside the carriages as the cold set hungry and thirsty patrons sprinting along the platforms. Refreshment rooms were like oases. Stoical women in green uniforms were stationed behind large battered tea urns and pots, poised to dispense pies, rock cakes and stiff-with-the-frost ham sandwiches. The 'refreshment girls' developed a special mid-1950s persona. Peter Cape wrote a song, 'Taumarunui on the Main Trunk Line', that chronicled the fixation of a northern paramour with a refreshment room 'sheila' based in Taumarunui. It was a catchy tune and a believable lyric, but the fact was that many refreshment girls stationed along the main trunk married local locomotive drivers who shared similar twilight zone working hours and understood the other side of midnight.

Forty-five minutes are set aside for train crews to change over and passengers from both trains to partake of a decent nosh-up in the station café, with the towering mountains close at hand. The wind whistles across the tussocked plains, engendering keen appetites. The café fare, contemporary to a fault, does not include mince pies, rock cakes, ham sandwiches or mustard-doctored coffee.

As the mountain mist drifts over the station you are more likely to find panini, muffins, quiche, red and white wine, and coffee ranging from flat white to latte. You can't help but notice that the sudden inundation of passengers seeking sustenance results in jostling queues, a bit like the old refreshment stop stampedes, although the 45-minute stop helps to prevent an exact replica.

The train drifts north. Even before the panini has settled we begin threading down the Raurimu Spiral. Train staff are now talking us through our descent of the world-famous Spiral. It's a remarkable engineering feat and never fails to amaze me, regardless of how many times I've taken the plunge. It was designed in the 1890s by R.W. Holmes, the senior engineer of the Public Works Department, and is made up of two tunnels, three horseshoe curves and one complete circle.

It's all about negotiating the Waimarino Plateau and the need for the line to proceed while plummeting 500 m in little more than 25 km. The Raurimu Spiral itself covers 6.8 km and is a wondrous and highly entertaining diversion, a slow rail rollercoaster ride through the bush with the Main Trunk zig-zagging from up to down as we head north.

There have been instances of sleeping passengers waking somewhere along the spiral's corkscrewing course and becoming convinced that they are on the wrong train — the one heading the other way. Another sort of serious disorientation occurred during the construction of the Spiral, in hardnosed, pioneering days when construction workers ferried dynamite 'within their shirts'. In winter dynamite was considered 'susceptible to impact' and thus it was that one railway ganger was killed. Amazingly, given the gung-ho approach of the rail construction workers, many of whom were ex gold-miners from Queensland, Waihi and the West Coast of the South Island, along with

As the Overlander penetrates the mountain-studded centre of the North Island, the mystique of New Zealand's longest passenger train journey closes in like the foothills.

sundry English, Irish and 'negroes', this was one of the few fatalities.

Within the Raurimu community, as the Spiral took shape, several characters emerged. Geoff the chef claimed he had prepared a 12-course meal for the King of Portugal, yet he became notorious for his burnt soup. Fellow construction workers came up with an asbestos mat to absorb the heat of the wood-fired ovens. Better soup should have been the outcome, but Geoff the chef conjured up an other-worldly taste by placing the mat in the soup pot, under the soup bones.

As night fell over the bush, construction workers in their camp would banish the dark by lighting candles fashioned out of fat from the few mutton carcasses that made it up to the construction site. Meanwhile in Raurimu township, which housed 1000 people at the height of the Spiral's construction, illegal games of two-up kept the lawless element busy.

'That there Raurimu Spiral is one of the world's great rail features,' an older American guy — Les from Dayton,

Ohio — declares. I remember him gesturing with his soup spoon towards the peaks of Ruapehu, Ngauruhoe and Tongariro in the National Park café.

'I'd always wanted to do what we did back in '99,' Les drawls as the Overlander speeds away from Raurimu Station at the base of the Spiral.

'We hunkered down in an old bushman's hut next to the Main Trunk, back up the Spiral, and watched the trains pass, going north and south. We were surrounded by dense wet bush in the very heart of what you guys call the heartland, where the only sounds came from the throats of native birds, and the throb of engines as they mounted the grade no more than 50 metres from the front window. Nowadays of course electric engines have taken the place of steam and diesel. God knows what it must have been like in the days before this section of the main trunk was electrified.'

One of the advantages of undertaking a long train ride is the opportunity to enjoy the company of fellow travellers, perfect strangers, although as Leroy, a younger, loose-limbed American observes, some are less perfect than others.

We first came across Leroy in the back of the buffet area as the train crawled past Horopito, the site of 'Smash Palace', a car graveyard that featured in some of the more robust moments of movies like *Smash Palace* and *Goodbye Pork Pie* during that period of New Zealand film that was once described as 'Central North Island Gothic'.

Leroy or Elroy, or it might have been just plain Roy, was from the deep south. Hattiesburg, Mississippi. His drawl took me by surprise, hence the Leroy/Elroy/Roy confusion.

Somewhere along the line a gregarious fellow, a

Hamiltonian like myself, called Hamish has made himself known. Our point of reference is the emergence at Palmerston North of a huge man I figured was Gary Knight, one of New Zealand's best former rugby prop forwards. Hamish, a fellow rugby fan, swears black and blue that the wide-shouldered specimen ordering an all-day breakfast at the buffet was Keith Murdoch, a reclusive and highly controversial ex All-Black prop who was banished from a tour of Great Britain.

Eventually, both of us are proved wrong. The all-day breakfaster (he polished off another two between Owhango and Taumarunui) eventually gravitated into our company, courtesy of another Welshman, Owen of Llanelli, who had been drawn into the contentions Hamish and I were hammering out in the rear observation car. As magnificent mountain views recede, matters rugby take on a certain intensity. Owen, a former first-grade loose forward, is able to settle the mistaken identity prop-forward conundrum by introducing his all-day breakfast travelling companion Barry Griffiths, a former Pontypridd and Wales B International, who, up close, looks nothing like Gary Knight or Keith Murdoch.

As the central North Island mountains disappear on the horizon, the man-mountain Barry and his chirpy, lilting companion Owen, prove convivial and amusing travelling companions. By the time the Overlander eases its way out of the King Country heartland, a certain bond has been established.

As the Overlander penetrates the mountain-studded centre of the North Island, the mystique of New Zealand's longest passenger train journey closes in like the foothills.

Night trains used to thunder through here in the old days. If you were lucky a clear winter's night would present moonlit vistas of snowdrifts extending all the way to the stark outlines of the mountains. The old steam-heated expresses and limiteds were like incubated capsules as they raced across the frozen flatlands of the central plateau.

Manunui, almost a dormitory town now, sees the Main Trunk head due west to Taumarunui, a few kilometres further on. Taumarunui still feels like an archetypal King Country railway town. You expect to see fired-up relief steam engines waiting in the yard.

Taumarunui, as gateway to the Whanganui River and the Whanganui National Park, takes on an added dimension these days. The park has a mystical aspect as the expanding Whanganui River tumbles into steep gorges and broken, bush-fringed country west of the town. A vast tract of lowland forest, one of the densest in the North Island, dominates the park, which is home to teeming birdlife including the brown kiwi, tui and kereru, the native pigeon.

Passengers alight at Taumarunui to join canoe, kayak and jetboat rides down the river and into the park, visiting features like the Bridge to Nowhere, a large concrete edifice built to access and develop the town and valley of Mangapurua after World War I. The remote location and difficulty of access led to the collapse of the Mangapurua dream, although the bridge, opened in 1936, has stood the test of time.

Further downstream the Whanganui River road accompanies the river from Pipiriki to the main highway leading to the city of Wanganui. River steamers continued on this stretch after the river became impassable beyond Pipiriki. (In the old days steamers used to ply the Whanganui waters all the way from Wanganui to Taumarunui). In the early 1970s a communal settlement at Jerusalem was established by poet James K. Baxter. Earlier, in 1892, Mother Mary Joseph Aubert, established the first community of sisters, a religious order, at Jerusalem.

Taumarunui may yet become a critical rail junction. It used to be. Back in the 1960s the Auckland to New Plymouth railcar touched base with Taumarunui Station before heading north again, beyond Okahukura, into the lonely recesses of inland Taranaki.

The rail journey from Taumarunui to Stratford plunged into the unknown. The line through inland Taranaki was isolated even by day. Towering valley walls and twisting river gorges presented problems to rail construction gangs, and by night, the railcar ride through such lonely outposts presented recesses that were as black and forsaken as on any New Zealand Rail route. Ohura station was well-lit though. The lights were a welcome relief after the ominous darkness. The railcar continued swaying through the valleys, past Tahora and Whangamomona.

Eventually, on that journey, we reached New Plymouth at 2.00 am. The wind whistled off Mt Taranaki. I wandered around and found a bed and breakfast arrangement, where the proprietress agreed that the rail service on the Taumarunui–New Plymouth route was not all it could be. I awoke to the sound of the Tasman Sea crashing on the coastline and wondered for more than a minute how I had ever got there.

Despite the diminished and diminishing services on the Taumarunui-Stratford branch, the fact that the line is not just an inconsequential spur (it covers 143.49 km and features 24 tunnels), and the dawning awareness that rail options need to be factored into New Zealand's developing transport needs in the era of global warming and climate change, could see Taumarunui resurrected as a rail junction hub.

Taumarunui is a friendly, positive place despite its recent privations. Located at the confluence of the fledgling Whanganui River and the Ongarue, it is also the commencement point of the Lost World Highway, State Highway 43, that meanders and winds to Taranaki. The Overlander doesn't stay here long, unlike the old refreshment-stop days. In fact the duration of the whistlestop is gauged by the time it takes the average smoker to reduce one king-size filter tip cigarette to ashes on the platform.

According to PA announcements, the stretch between Taumarunui and Te Kuiti is regarded by train staff as the 'hard yards' of the northward journey. There are no longer mountains or viaducts to create diversions, but the land presents a special character just the same.

A few kilometres north of Taumarunui the Okahukura junction settlement sees the inland Taranaki line swing across the Ongarue River and disappear into the mysterious rural backblocks.

The Main Trunk follows the course of the Ongarue River, past Okahukura with its distinctive road-rail bridge. Rail junctions are usually bustling places, but this one is as quiet as the slow-flowing Ongarue. State Highway 4, the main road north from Taumarunui, keeps us company. Its

SUVs and truck and trailer units are strangely reassuring. When I was young and living in Te Kuiti I figured the only way to travel south through this rugged heartland was to catch a train. So much local folklore hinted at the impenetrability of the interior and I was young enough to think that roads couldn't get through.

A few kilometres further onward the remnants of the once bustling Ongarue settlement represent the last evidence of concentrated population for some time. Ongarue used to be the junction point with the Main Trunk of the Ongarue Ellis and Burnard Tramway. In days when men were men and miles were not yet kilometres, the Ongarue Tramway wound through the bush for 23 miles. It retains a reputation as being the most spectacular and indeed the last of this kind of timber servicing line. It even had its own spiral and came to invigorate the township of Ongarue, which boasted a rugby team and more than a handful of houses.

The major 1958 floods damaged the bush tramway so badly it was never re-opened. All that survived was the one-mile section from the mill to Ongarue Station, at a time when the economic efficiency of log extraction and finite nature of the timber resource itself dictated closure terms.

There are stretches of the Overlander course that cover some of the more relentless backblock sectors of New Zealand. Population density dies. Green hills and grey bluffs fill the horizon. When towns appear along the track, they seem like cities. Taumarunui and Te Kuiti, substantial towns by backblocks reckoning, dominate river valleys, yet they are set apart by miles of lonely ramparts, sweeping hills and scattered sheep.

Deserted wooden houses moulder on hillsides or take on an afterlife as haybarns. The roofs of woolsheds and farm buildings glisten off to the west of the track as the train edges around cuttings sliced into the sides of hills Australians might call mountains — part of some great dividing range.

A four-wheel-drive vehicle can be seen kicking up dust on a tributary road that snakes back God knows where into the hills. Homesteads with bright, bungalowed facades look down over valleys and ridges. Out here the thin-on-the-ground locals tend not to wave at the train. It's as if you have disturbed their solitude, or could be privy to some gothic, ritualistic vigil.

The train purrs as it negotiates these hidden reaches. It is mid-afternoon and several travellers nod off. The backblocks are soporific. The red wine, in some cases, has had its effect.

The line leaves the highway to its own devices beyond the settlement of Ongarue, and although a road of sorts remains on our shoulder, it's a token gesture. Waimiha is desolate, yet ruggedly beautiful. The Pureora Forest Park looms to the east. Tumbledown buildings, abandoned, sinking marsh-bound machinery, and boarded-up bungalows usher the Overlander on.

The Pureora Forest Park survived the threat of clearfelling forestry in the 1970s. Protest action saw the habitat of the rare North Island kokako remain largely intact. Although there is little in the way of public transport to the park, many tourists with hired cars access the Totara Walk, Mount Pureora Summit Track and the Rimu Walk through the ancient forest noted for its stands of native trees like matai, rimu, tawa and kahikatea. The Pouakani Tree, the largest totara in New Zealand, is a star performer.

At Poro-o-tarao an infamous tunnel awaits. It's fine now, having been reconfigured and expanded to accommodate the Main Trunk overhead electric catenary, but in the old days the tunnel was approached with dread. When steam was still king, train crews used to suffer from soot and smoke as KAs and ABs buffeted through the narrow cleavage which leaked copiously and was always regarded as being too tight a fit.

I realise I haven't told any of my travelling companions that I will be getting off at Te Kuiti. There is a hurried shaking of hands as the train eases down the Waitete embankment, past the old cement works, beyond Rugby Park (still don't know why it hasn't been re-named Colin Meads Park, or Meads Park, or Pinetree Park after the man who is arguably New Zealand's most famous living All Black), past the intricately carved and substantial Te Tokanganui-a-noho marae and the huge, stooping statue of the sheep shearer.

The Overlander doesn't dally at Te Kuiti any more. There is a late afternoon flurry of farewells and welcomes, a rapid exchange of baggage. The lowering sun shafts light through the station apertures that open on to the main street, and half blinds anyone trying to catch a familiar face.

This is a familiar place. It's still basically the same old station. I still expect Albert the porter to be scampering about, parched passengers moving with intent toward the refreshment rooms and clusters of schoolboys, of whom I used to be one all those years ago, eating fish and chips of dubious quality and waving at the faces of the pretty girls peering from the carriage windows at a town they no doubt remained perplexed about. Why would anyone want to come from — certainly remain in — such a quiet backwater?

As I wave goodbye to my travelling companions — the decidedly un-pretty Welsh faces of Owen and Barry, the angular grimacing Hamish and, yes, there's Leroy at last rotating his baseball cap, and giving a Yankee thumbs up, I know exactly why people would want to come from and indeed remain in such an apparent outpost, now just a 'minor' stop on the Overlander route.

As the train bucks slightly before heading north I stand alone on the deserted platform. A fox terrier cocks its leg against a platform support and the signals change from red to green to red — not because of the fox terrier's actions but simply because time changes everything and change, however arbitrary and wanton, has its time. Te Kuiti is a good place to be, like all hometowns.

⑫ FROM TURNTABLE JUNCTION TO THE BRIGHT LIGHTS OF BRITOMART: THE OVERLANDER

TE KUITI TO AUCKLAND

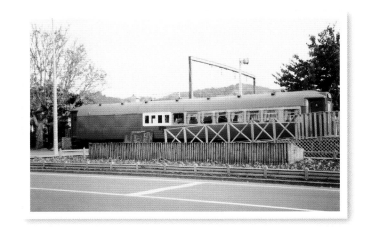

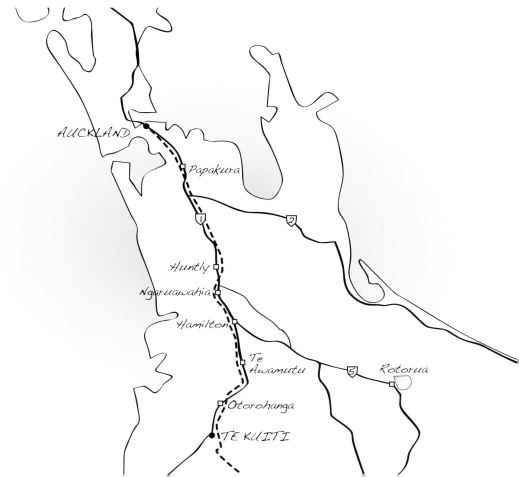

T e Kuiti was not just a major stop on the Main Trunk line in the old days. By local reckoning it was also a junction. As the Main Trunk south began to climb the Waitete bank just beyond the marae, a branch line of sorts carried on along the flat to serve the limeworks, cement works and saleyards and, it was suggested, Rugby Park on match day, before backing up, the AB engine in reverse, all the way north to Te Kuiti station.

PREVIOUS PAGE Where the old Te Kuiti piecart used to be, a converted railway carriage now performs the same function, while honouring the town's rail heritage.

Nowadays the Te Kuiti piecart is an old converted railway carriage. Taumarunui has a café honouring the same rail artefact. The Te Kuiti piecart meshes with the restored station and enhanced approaches that tip their hat to the town's railway heritage. It's just a matter now of honouring the present: Te Kuiti's ideal location to welcome more passenger trains to the North Island's heartland. My old mate Bill and I discussed the rail future of the town over the traditional steak and eggs while hunkered down in the carriage piecart, as Te Kuiti on a Friday night exploded around us. Freight trains thundered past a few metres away to the west. Boy racers, both of them, doughnutted in the main street off to the north-east. Teenagers and half-cut stock agents clustered around the piecart servery like hungry moths. In that respect nothing had changed in 40 years, although we both agreed the quality of the steak had come along in leaps and bounds. The stock agents could perhaps take a collective bow. Indeed the revival of the meat industry in the Te Kuiti area has been a local success story. Such an achievement is doubly meritorious, being associated with an area of endeavour that has, for so long and over vast stretches of the heartland, seen the heart cut out of meat processing plants — the old freezing works.

Te Kuiti has a turntable in its station yards too. It was a long time coming. The idea was floated in recent years when it was determined that a turntable would mean excursion trains could be turned at Te Kuiti. The town that owed its existence to the railways would see its future enhanced by trainloads of northerners, flush with cash, being deposited at the old rail centre and released for a few hours to expand the wallets of local shopkeepers and hoteliers before heading north again, behind a turned loco, with empty pockets and fond memories of a town resurrected. Te Kuiti would not just be the shearing capital; it would be a 'minor' stop on the Main Trunk transformed into an excursion rail centre fit to foot it with any.

When the Muster Express of 1993 came to Te Kuiti, before the turntable, the impact on the town was profound. Gareth Hewitt, an old friend, had a stall that sold garden furniture and he was happy to record significant profits on the basis of 300 northerners wandering up Rora Street with money to burn and nowhere else to turn. The turntable was in operation when the Waitomo Centenary train in 2004 introduced hundreds more. The hope now is that Te Kuiti will cash in on the turntable and excursion trains will come on a regular basis. All it needs is promotion and an inclination to rekindle the dream. Perhaps the trains could be named the Meads Express or the Pinetree Limited after the famous rugby player. It seems just a matter of taking advantage of a living Kiwi legend, and a priceless history as a pivotal railway centre and junction.

After a Friday night in Te Kuiti it's time to head north again. The Overlander glides to a stop pretty much on time. I am allocated a seat after being told by the jovial train manager that I can sit wherever I like as long as it isn't on the driver's knee. The train pulls out of the upgraded station with its new turntable and is soon heading north at a useful clip.

The Overlander continues to gather speed now that it's beyond the rugged ramparts of the real King Country. The train is also beyond the summer speed restrictions imposed because high temperatures in the inland recesses threaten to buckle the rails. Not that any passenger services have jumped the tracks in the past. I can't recall expresses and limiteds having to cut back on speed just because temperatures touched 30 degrees in the old days.

Mind you, we didn't have OSH and ACC and politically correct environmental watchdogs back then. Most trains got through, although a case could be mounted that the terrible Tangiwai disaster might have been prevented had there been an OSH mentality abroad in the 1950s. And of course the use of continuous welded track makes buckling more likely in 2007.

Otorohanga, 20 km north of Te Kuiti, is a tidy town these days. It prides itself on being New Zealand's Kiwiana capital, although it is more widely known as the base for the Kiwi House Native Bird Park, where the lifestyles of the kiwi and many other New Zealand native birds and wildlife, including the prehistoric tuatara, are on display.

Otorohanga is also the main portal for travellers wishing to visit the world-famous Waitomo Caves. Several passengers alight on the strength of the connection.

The Waitomo Caves are one of New Zealand's best known tourist attractions. They were always there, as the King Country was opened up to European incursion, but it took the inquisitiveness of Maori chief Tane Tinorau and English surveyor Fred Mace in 1887, utilising only candle power, to discover the labyrinth of underground waterways, caverns and glow-worm grottos, before reporting back to a disbelieving world.

Initially Tane Tinorau guided interested parties through the caves but, in the nature of the paternalistic, monocultural New Zealand government of the day, the authorities took over the caves' operation and developed the site. It was only in 1989 that some recompense was made in terms of Maori ownership, and now the indigenous people receive a percentage of all revenue accruing from the natural wonder and take an active part in its management and administration.

The Waikato Glow-worm Caves and the Aranui Caves are the most popular attractions, the former featuring clusters of glow-worms viewed during a surreal boat ride, after visitors have clambered through limestone chambers replete with stalactites and stalagmites. The Aranui Caves are marked by high-ceilinged caverns and limestone formations perhaps even more spectacular than the glow-worm caves.

Over the years the Waitomo Caves hinterland has developed tourist attractions that would not have emerged but for the location of the caves. Adventure caving, cave tubing or blackwater rafting (simply because it all happens underground), and abseiling down great limestone-gorged cleavages in the land, have attracted a new wave of adrenalin tourists.

Soon the Overlander is hurtling towards the Waikato region across the rich dairy flatlands.

Mount Kakapuku, a rare protrusion on the plains near the border of the King Country and the Waikato, has been a point of reference for years. The Overlander skirts the green dome as the shark-toothed Mount Pirongia dominates the western horizon.

Mt Pirongia was a strategic peak during the New Zealand Wars and many trenches dug into the mountainside can still be sighted along the walkways of Pirongia Forest Park, accessible from Te Awamutu, or more appropriately, Otorohanga, for that is where the Overlander now stops.

The Land Wars of the 1860s were a seemingly inevitable clash between the indigenous people of New Zealand and the European settlers, out to make a new life for themselves as farmers and small allotment holders in territory that was already spoken for. Some of the most dramatic clashes occurred in the Waikato, in regions now traversed by the Main Trunk line.

Te Awamutu was originally a garrison town for government forces and one of the most remarkable battles occurred at Orakau pa in Kihikihi where 2,000 soldiers were stymied for several days by a defiant clutch of 300 Maori.

After the rugged, often claustrophobic hills of the central King Country, to rattle across the Puniu River into the Waikato is to concede to the land of the cow. Milk is regarded as white gold in this part of New Zealand, nowhere more so than in the town and surroundings of Te Awamutu.

Until the 1880s the Puniu River represented the limit of European expansion south, especially with regard to the extension of the North Island Main Trunk. In 1885 the river was the location of the turning of the first sod in laying the Te Awamutu to Marton section of line that would complete the long link between Auckland and Wellington.

Te Awamutu Station was always located an awkward distance from the centre of town. In that sense it was never a typical railway settlement along the lines of Taumarunui and Te Kuiti. That has counted against it, for now the Overlander doesn't even stop at the remnants of a station. Yet Te Awamutu, home town of the Finn brothers, arguably New Zealand's favourite rock musicians (both through their solo work and through the bands Split Enz and Crowded House), is an attractive, prosperous place

OPPOSITE Te Awamutu in days when the dairying stronghold had a functional station.

with a reputation as New Zealand's Rosetown, thanks to its excellent rose gardens. Te Awamutu has an undeserved reputation for smugness, although most people here are friendly. It's all perhaps to do with old money generated from dairy dollars, and those who serve an establishment based on confiscated Maori land. A mischievous writer once pointed the finger at Te Awamutu's 'rude merchants', shopkeepers who only had to be pleasant to the 'right folk', and said that if he served the wealthy cockies, even the village idiot could become a millionaire.

Hamilton is still unjustly underrated as a city. Because it's so close to Auckland travellers tend to overlook it, and then there is its landlocked situation. Yet it sits astride the slow-flowing, handsome Waikato River and boasts a picturesque lake (Rotoroa), factors that should anchor any water-loving tourist. Climatically, there's little to stop things growing in Hamilton. The sprawling Hamilton Gardens and several spacious parks are among New Zealand's best. A trip on the *Waipa Delta*, a paddle steamer that chugs up and down the Waikato, and time out to visit the Museum of Art and History are stylish features of a stopover in New Zealand's largest inland settlement.

In June each year, despite its often fog-bound setting at Mystery Creek, the agricultural extravaganza known as the Field Days draws thousands of locals and outsiders. Special trains often serve the event and Hamilton restaurateurs and publicans rub their hands together at the financial prospects. The agricultural heart of New Zealand pumps powerfully, confirming Hamilton as the rural service town that grew on the back of the commercial success of farming into the country's fourth largest city.

After wandering along the platform to watch the diesel loco take over from the electric (electrification terminates at Hamilton), I scramble back on board. I contemplate the eastern platform of Hamilton Station, the one that serves the Bay of Plenty line and the underground central city station, deemed to be unsafe because of bouts of vandalism. It's still there, mothballed, the only New Zealand underground city station, if you don't count the Britomart lightshow in Auckland.

What a thousand pities that was. A genuine central city underground station that could have been the focus for suburban rail services that, had some city father or mother grasped the nettle, would now see Hamilton spared the gridlock for which Auckland is famous.

'There don't seem to be many trains,' Clive, the Englishman occupying the window seat adjacent to me, reckons.

He is becoming agitated by the fact that Hamilton Station, despite being a junction, shows little activity on the Bay of Plenty line.

'It's a farce,' says Clive. 'Bay of Plenty indeed. A perfectly good junction but not a case of plenty of trains. A dubious junction, in fact.'

'This station, or more accurately, Frankton just up the line, used to be a hive of activity. It had refreshment rooms too.'

I continue to contemplate the refreshment room phenomenon. Recently I read an account of All Black Jack Finlay, who came to grief on Frankton Station just after World War II. Finlay wrote himself off and out of a rugby test match against Australia when he came smartly into contact with an open window on the station platform while running for sustenance at the refreshment rooms. It was a uniquely Kiwi, post-war way to invalidate yourself out of a test match.

Despite Jack Finlay's mishap there are grounds to suppose that the refreshment room rush should be re-enacted on a regular basis. These days you get the feeling that a lot of young travellers and tourists have been rather spoiled by onboard catering arrangements. The rush provided by white water rafting and bungy jumping might be duplicated if, on reaching specified refreshment stops, young tourists had five minutes to plunge down the platform, avoiding strategically placed obstacles, join the ruck at the counter, lunge at the dwindling stocks of authentic rail food and then sprint back to the train with hot pies, rock cakes and scalding tea or coffee. It could become New Zealand's answer to the running of the bulls at Pamplona.

Meanwhile on the Overlander I buy a coffee from the buffet. Following squally weather the skies are now clearing and the sinking sun bathes the paddocks with opaque yellow light. My need for coffee overrides any sense of personal safety and I strip the cover off the hot coffee in an attempt to hasten the cooling process. At that moment one of the train staff, witnessing my wanton violation of what is probably an OSH-inspired safety device, castigates me, gently enough, for not only endangering myself but also those seated nearby. What if the train hit a cow? Would there not be scalding coffee raining down? Good point, I concede, but wouldn't it make more sense to avoid the cow in the first place? Anyway, back in the old days a hot deluge of tea or coffee from a good old Railways china cup toughened you up. At the very least it heightened your ability to keep an eye out for such dangers. Now we are so protected our reflexes and instincts for survival have atrophied. But point taken. Fair enough. I ease the top back on the coffee container and thank the staff member for her concern.

'I didn't realise I was in such danger,' Clive the Englishman jibes.

'She's right. There are a lot of cows around. This is the Waikato after all.'

The hosts and hostesses on the Overlander are a far cry from the heartland guards of old. They are uniformly well-informed, solicitous and attractively uniformed. The old guards used to wear dark, sandpaper garb. They were always men. Nothing to do with sexism. That didn't come along until light years later. They were part of a parochial, patriarchal, regimented society, an extension really of the police force and armed services.

Woe betide anyone who didn't have a ticket back then. But then again guards, although gruff, could also show great generosity. A tall tale might see you right. For example, there was the time just out of Taumarunui, when the guard found you had no document to punch.

'So you're telling me your ticket fell out of your back pocket going through the Poro-o-tarao tunnel?'

'Yes sir. It happened so quickly.'

'Must have done. We don't reach Poro-o-tarao for another half hour. Don't do it again, son.' The guard would invariably grunt on such occasions, making reference to the fact that he was young once too, before shuffling on and punching tickets through the carriage.

The Overlander, in the background, passes through Te Rapa marshalling yards on the outskirts of Hamilton.

OPPOSITE The remains of the day's sun refract as the Overlander commences its last hours northward.

storm in the night and now, in the breaking light of dawn, were crying out for a dry change.

Steam engines had other uses too. In the depths of the King Country where the lights of lonely farm houses took on the appearance of scattered glow-worms, the train crew used to fry up an early cooked breakfast on a coal shovel that was edged closer to the fire box until the eggs, bacon and sausages were sizzling nicely. If there was a modicum of ash on the sausages it was a small price to pay.

It's a shame the Overlander doesn't do a modern-day, ash-tinged version of shovel-fired bacon, eggs and sausages, but the 'all day breakfast' I attack as the train passes through Ngaruawahia and over the Waikato River bridge, is true to its claim. It's 5.30 in the afternoon.

The Overlander is running smoothly northward. Passengers, including a healthy smattering of children and babies, have settled down for the final hour or so of the journey when the peace is disturbed by a pot-gutted cell phone operator. Booming-voiced, self-absorbed, he informs us all that he is some sort of agricultural contractor returning from Wellington, having put his case to a select committee. Perhaps he has driven a tractor up the Beehive steps the way Shane Ardern the MP did. He seems the type.

'A flightless but noisy Kiwi,' Clive mutters as we learn more about 'Butch' and 'Grinder'.

'Exactly, mate. Tell Grinder to piss off. What was the damage anyway? A stuffed flange? Yeah. Right. Yeah-nah. Right. Look, Butch. What!'

Cell phones. The contractor was now pacing the corridor of the train, invading everyone's space. So much

There's more vigilance now although the train staff lack the gruffness. The old guards wouldn't dream of providing a running commentary on the history of the line. The fact is, they were part of that history. They wouldn't come to your aid when drunks stumbled and slurred up the aisle and, making eye contact, crashed into the seat next to you, demanding your total attention. But they were protective of women and children. Some trains pulled into stations with babies' nappies flapping out the fireman's window. The guard in such situations had provided a nappy-drying service for young mothers whose bouncers had weed up a

concern these days about privacy issues and here's this lumbering, slack-jowelled aficionado of new technology letting us in on sensitive commercial details.

'You tell that bloody Grinder that tax evasion is not just an option, it's a bloody right. Right? Yeah-nah.'

An Asian tourist enters the carriage hoping to advance in the opposite direction to Red the Neck, but finds his path blocked by banality.

'Excuse,' the tourist pleads.

Red, seemingly unaware that anyone else could possibly be occupying the earth's surface, does not respond.

'Excuse, prease,' the Asian persists, raising his voice.

'That digger goes for at least a hundred bucks an hour. Nothing less. You tell Grinder that's the going rate. Yeah-nah. You tell him to pull his effing head in.'

Red is now facing the Asian man in one of those dissociated moments when a person talking on a cell phone in a crowded environment gives the impression he is talking to you.

'No swear, prease,' the tourist, now nose to nose or more precisely, nose to neck with Red, pleads.

You have to hand it to the hostess. Coming across the confrontation she skilfully averts any fallout with a few hushed words. Red terminates his call. The Asian man squeezes past, returning to his seat at the head of the carriage.

The cell phone kerfuffle has diverted passengers from passing vistas, although it has to be admitted that the territory between the northern Hamilton industrial suburbs and the small town of Ngaruawahia is more mundane than most. Ngaruawahia is a distinctive town though, dominated by rivers. The Waipa flows into the mighty Waikato a short distance from the rail bridge which in turn is located downriver from the sprawling Turangawaewae Marae, home of the Maori King movement and residence of the current Maori King.

His predecessor, Te Arikinui Dame Te Atairangikaahu died in 2006. The train no longer stops at Ngaruawahia, but on the occasion of the Maori Queen's death, special trains rained down on the centre of her influence. Turangawaewae Marae represents an aspect of New Zealand that is unique, a movement that represents an indigenous people who have retained their identity and their dignity.

Conversation dries up as the watery aspect of the magnificent Waikato River comes into view. Sacred Taupiri Mountain, the Maori burial site, is festooned with flowers and ornaments of remembrance. The train runs adjacent to the wide, languid river for several kilometres. It is almost lake-like where the tall smoke stacks of Huntly Power Station jut above the river. I notice a line of houses I've never seen before, their back decks nudging the river like the lakeside communities on Lake Pontchartrain, coming in to New Orleans from the north. Perhaps some old trees have been removed or, as is so often the case with train travel, there is always something new to see even on familiar routes.

The Waikato River is New Zealand's longest, beginning its journey as the Tongariro River beyond the southern entry point into Lake Taupo, through which it flows, before bursting out of New Zealand's largest lake and setting off through cleavages like the Huka Falls. The hydro dams between Taupo and Cambridge slow its flow but by the time it reaches Ngaruawahia and the rail bridge that carries the Overlander over it, the Waikato has expanded again into its unencumbered, slow-flowing surge to the north.

The river was busy with Maori waka in the days when produce grown on inland plots was transported as far as Tuakau before primitive road access relayed the cargoes to the growing town of Auckland. Past Tuakau the river bends westward towards its Tasman Sea coast outlet.

During the Land Wars, coal-fired gunboats struggled up the river to lend their weight to the conflict. Once the wars were over, the Waikato became an important communication link in the years before the Main Trunk railway went through.

Huntly is a town with a rich railway past and maybe something of a future, given that the junction line to the west, over the soaring river bridge, has been upgraded to carry coal trains from the mines at Rotowaro to the Main Trunk and up to the Glenbrook Steel Mill, via the Mission Bush branch. Perhaps, as a guy in a Hamilton secondhand bookshop suggested to me once, the Rotowaro branch will one day be reintegrated into the rail network as the setting for a passenger service.

Huntly also has a vintage railway, the Pukemiro Bush Tramway. Travellers could do worse than make the journey to Huntly with a view to travelling on this remarkable restored chunk of rail Kiwiana.

In recent years while travelling north, I've become aware of a line that disappears towards the east into the low hills as the houses of Huntly run out. At first I thought

it was a back-shunt of sorts, an extended siding still very much a part of the Main Trunk. Now I know it's a coalmine line and real trains run on it to Kimihia despite its rather spartan appearance. Being aware of its existence only hardens my resolve to stop over in Huntly one day and observe all the rail permutations of one of New Zealand's unsung railway settlements.

The lowering sun glances off the slow-flowing Waikato. After a wet spell it's riding high. An abandoned barge not far south of the bridge to Naike, an apparition that has been wedged on the far bank for as long as I can recall, is now being lapped by the river. It recalls another forsaken relic — the old Horotiu freezing works back down the track — that is now looking decidedly decrepit, with a section of the old woolstore looking like a Baghdad bombsite.

'Operational restrictions have been the cause of the slight delay in the running of this service,' the voice over the PA purrs. No problem.

We leave the road and river as the line seeks out its own course through the vast Whangamarino wetlands. Despite the darkening landscape it is perfectly obvious that we have entered a unique netherworld, complete with distinctive, dense vegetation, limpid pools and teeming birdlife.

I recall many years ago being perplexed by the way one prong of the Main Trunk — double-tracked at this stage — forked away like a genuine branch line. Back then I would have suggested that there was in fact another line in this neck of the woods. In subsequent years, it dawned on me that the Main Trunk double track split at one point

Pukemiro Bush Tramway runs trains that resemble main trunk services of a hundred years ago.

simply because the wetlands made it hard to find solid ground on which to secure two tracks.

Soon enough we rejoin the road and river as Whangamarino recedes.

Other passengers have been pleasantly surprised by our plunge through the wetlands. It remains one of the unsung highlights of this stretch of the main trunk. The Whangamarino wetlands are the most extensive in New Zealand and worthy of the level of interest they have generated among many Overlander passengers. I can't speak for Clive, who seems displaced. Perhaps he had a bad experience in some steaming South American delta in colonial days. He seems old enough and sufficiently global to have lost his way at some point in a dense, virtually impenetrable stretch, with anacondas dangling from the trees above pools bubbling with razor-toothed caymans and piranhas.

The sun seems to be taking its time setting. A lingering Franklin County dusk, complete with moving shadows and filtered light, accompanies us for several miles. The train is surprisingly quiet again. The children on board seem worn out by the sheer magnitude of the journey from Wellington.

A stocky man wearing shorts in April is looking a bit restless though. Don't tell me we have another redneck in the ranks. At Mercer his bare legs begin swaying almost involuntarily out into the aisle. It's obviously been a long day for him too. Eventually, as the train negotiates the sharp westward shift beyond Pokeno he settles for a rapidly consumed all day breakfast and a shot of bourbon.

Paerata is one of those rail precincts that used to have

a sense of mystery. If I didn't know that the Mission Bush branch angles away from the Main Trunk at this point — and further away on a 5.5-km spur at Glenbrook, off the old Waiuku branch, to the steel mill — I'd be dying to know what that junction line was all about. I'm almost obsessive about having a handle on every conceivable branch or spur or industrial siding. It's got a lot to do with the fact that New Zealand's rail system is not vast. When travelling by train through America, Britain, Europe and even Australia, I could never hope to master the myriad networks. That knowledge brings its own comfort. In New Zealand, however, you feel a sense of responsibility to map out and become familiar with every steel highway.

Mind you, my awareness of the significance of Paerata Junction is reasonably recent. Coal trains from Huntly and lime trains from Hangatiki use the branch to feed the hungry Pacific Steel Mills. I have learned that there used to be a mixed goods passenger service via Paerata that went all the way to Waiuku. The Glenbrook Vintage Railway, a must-see for any rail fan and, indeed, everyday tourist or holidaymaker, utilises a significant chunk of the old Waiuku branch. At one magical point the Mission Bush industrial branch and the Glenbrook tracks run virtually parallel to one another for a spell, creating a unique rail feature.

And of course Paerata, with all that rail activity down the line to the west, is suitably anonymous: a lonely New Zealand junction settlement in the middle of nowhere. Ironically, just a few miles up the track the famous Auckland urban sprawl kicks in. Eventually Paerata will be enveloped by houses and industrial installations, a more fitting setting for a rail junction. I receive a strange look as I make this point to a middle-aged woman who has joined the train at Pukekohe. She is determined to organise her meal tray and take advantage of onboard catering services before we reach Auckland. It's a matter of principle. The woman continues to insist on assembling her tray herself, despite a fumbling approach. I have her cased as a furiously independent and self-reliant person. There is something about the long, grey-blonde hair done up in a bun, the fierce blue eyes. She reminds me of Judy Collins, the folk singer, or any number of old hippie souls who never sold out. I thought women of her generation traded up, got made over, renounced the commune for Pakuranga and the gridlocked lifestyle before becoming yuppies in the 1980s and eventually CEOs or minions of the Crown. I may be wrong. We don't discuss such issues at any length.

It all comes down to the meal tray. It is not a friendly piece of apparatus. A heavy, ungainly appendage, it seems at odds with the Overlander's otherwise smooth and easy operation.

These days the Overlander makes a stop at Middlemore Hospital, where towering well-lit wards rise above us. Years ago the expresses thundered straight through, in the days when hospitals and other unsettling institutions tended to be hidden from the public gaze.

By now we are locked into the South Auckland urban sprawl by night. These flickering suburbs help render Auckland one of the largest cities in the world in terms of area covered. Beyond Westfield you can feel the train swinging eastward, like an airliner banking. We are on

Auckland, this way, has one of the more picturesque rail approaches in New Zealand, even at night. The harbour aspect, with thousands of lights reflecting off the water as the rail bisects Hobson's Bay on a causeway, is breathtaking.

course for a spectacular arrival through the front door of the waterfront approach.

Auckland, this way, has one of the more picturesque rail approaches in New Zealand, even at night. The harbour aspect, with thousands of lights reflecting off the water as the rail bisects Hobson's Bay on a causeway, is breathtaking. The final run along the harbour's edge with the city skyline lit up, seemingly energising the train and drawing it onward like a moth to a flame, is suddenly terminated as we descend through a tunnel into the new Britomart Station to reach journey's end. The train empties rapidly. Passengers began preparing to alight almost as soon as the rural strangleholds receded and the Auckland suburbs set in. That was half an hour ago. Auckland's famous urban sprawl has deceived tourists into thinking that once there were no more farms out the window the train would be terminating its journey very soon.

Arriving at Britomart Station for the first time is a bit like entering the mother ship in the far reaches of space. Or an elaborate subterranean movie set. Initially it's hard to take it all in. There are the practicalities of uplifting luggage, meeting friends and family and saying farewell to fellow passengers. I shake hands with Clive as the Britomart lightshow pulses all around me.

There's a young Maori guy busking on the platform. The kid sings very well, his chord changes ring and echo as trains come and go. I drop two bucks into a cardboard box at his feet. 'Thanks, bro' is worked into the lyrics of 'Heart of Gold', a Neil Young song.

Half way up the escalator I see an Asian masseuse prodding a large fibrillating man behind a token fabric screen. Can't imagine New Zealand Rail providing such a service within the conservative chambers of the old Auckland Station. Strange blue light washes over everything and everybody as I seek out level two.

The upper level opening onto Queen Street houses several food outlets, a florist, an 'artist-in-residence' in vacant premises, ticket-sellers and information vendors. The food on offer is essentially Asian. No rock cakes, ham sandwiches or railway pies here. No ash-flecked bacon and eggs and sausages.

You could spend a couple of hours in Britomart, just taking in the 21st-century ambience. The artist-in-residence, the masseuse, the optical illusions created by zany lighting are just the tip of the iceberg. Wishing to immerse myself in the Britomart wonderland I descend the escalators.

The young Maori guy is now singing a U2 song — can't remember its name. There are now yawning gaps in my musical knowledge. I buy a basic paper cup of coffee from a tiny stall half-hidden at the foot of the escalator in the lounge-like lights of Britomart, and watch the suburban trains come and go.

Not too long ago stations in the middle of nowhere used to pop up at 2.00 am with all conventional lights blazing — oases on the Main Trunk providing sustenance and confirmation that you were not on a train heading for a black, silent oblivion. The lights of the refreshment room were especially dazzling as you lurched inside in a dream-like state, asking for a pie and a coffee.

We heard rumours that railway coffee had something in it. Something slightly illicit, like a habit-forming chemical that had you craving more coffee at Taihape, Palmerston North and Paekakariki and left you stumbling around Wellington Station looking for another fix in the cafeteria that wasn't always open when the overnight express got in. There were also reports that a pinch of something that curbed young men's urges as the train curved around cuttings, rammed through tunnels and cork-screwed up the Raurimu Spiral, had been flicked into the coffee, not unlike the stuff they slipped into soldiers' food to keep them docile.

Post-war speculation had it that we young bounders were being handled as if there was still a war on. A bit like barracks week and cadets at school. Marcus Lush in his popular TV programme, 'Off the Rails', highlighted what some people already suspected. Mustard was the mystery substance that found its way into railway coffee. I don't know if the chemical properties of mustard include the propensity to drown ardour, but I do recall a certain lack of 'romance of the railways' on long train journeys, even though young ladies sitting across the way could have been seen to be fetching in their clinging polo-neck jerseys and new-fangled, tight-fitting denim jeans — but for the doctored coffee.

The paper cup of flat white from the Britomart stall definitely had something in it. Caffeine. Despite the long journey north I felt recharged. I couldn't get enough of this new Kiwi rail environment. Wandering down the Britomart platforms is a step into the future. Passengers off the trains emerge from colourful shadows created by the merging kaleidoscope of floodlit walls. The stainless steel carriages reflect and often imitate the surrounding colours. Those lines from the Beatles' 'Lucy in the Sky with Diamonds' spring to mind again: 'Picture yourself on a train in a station, with plasticine porters with looking glass ties,' and 'The girl with kaleidoscope eyes.' I purchase another coffee. Perhaps there's something in it, in 2007, other than caffeine.

To a rail fan this is Hollywood, right here in the Queen city. Former Auckland mayor, Sir Dove-Myer Robinson, an avid advocate of urban train travel, can stop turning in his grave at last. The revolution has begun. Even now, a couple of years down the track so to speak, patronage of Auckland suburban services is on a dramatic rise. A new generation is finding the futuristic station compelling. I chat to one or two of them as they wait for trains at the end of their working day.

Jane is a young woman with kaleidoscope eyes who

lives in Newmarket. The train makes more sense and takes less time. Little more than ten minutes in fact. Her workmate Melodie lives out towards Waiuku in a renovated farmhouse and drives to Papakura in South Auckland every morning, where she catches an express suburban service to Britomart.

It wasn't always like this. Melodie used to live much closer to town in a correspondingly more expensive situation. Each morning she would endure the god-awful gridlock in a car that was costing her an arm and a leg.

Near the end of the line. The Auckland Skytower acts as a beacon for the Overlander.

Petrol prices and blood pressure levels escalated. Then she cottoned on to the idea of cheaper accommodation further out where she could take advantage of the greater frequency and increased efficiency of commuter trains.

This is an increasingly common story. As Aucklanders finally say no to the traffic congestion, the improved and improving rail commuter network has stepped up to the plate. Melodie and Jane know of several friends who have actually relocated so they can live within walking distance of a suburban railway station. Leaving the car in the garage is becoming a café talking point. Younger generations, who seem just as afflicted as my baby-boomer set with the delusion that they were the first tribe to discover coffee, alcohol and sex, are now claiming to have stumbled upon an ace new way to get from A to B — the train.

Take the train! And to go from Te Kuiti Station, with its faithful restoration and new turntable, harking back to the grand old days of steam and mustard in the coffee, to Britomart Station in 2007, has been a revelation. A time warp from the past to the future of New Zealand rail. In many ways it has been a leap of faith, but then much significant change happens when our eyes are closed.

Postscript

Considering the magnificence of the Overlander's stately meander through the heart of the North Island, linking the capital city Wellington with the country's largest conurbation, Auckland, it's almost impossible to accept that, at one sad stage in 2006 the train's total withdrawal was on the agenda. When that bizarre scenario is raised with foreign travellers, as the Overlander threads its way up the Raurimu Spiral, or crosses the many ornate viaducts, or skirts the central mountains, they smile benignly — you are either not well, or the information you're peddling is skewed.

Public outrage, a rare Kiwi commodity, signalled to those who had control over the fate of a New Zealand rail icon that a simple sacking of a service that represented New Zealand's past, present and future, would have long-term political, social and economic repercussions. Back to the drawing board. Brave new world market forces were forced to reconsider. The fate of the South Island's Southerner, now a dead duck, was not about to be repeated. Mistakes were seen to have been learned from, concessions made. The Overlander was saved, as much because ostrich-like Kiwis finally got out of their cars and patronised the endangered train, as because tourist operators and tourists themselves expressed unreserved disgust and made a point of travelling on a service that traversed a famous line through one of the world's most scenic regions.

Yet the Overlander is not operating to its potential. Eventually, it was deemed by boardroom lackeys that New Zealand's most important train would be free to operate on a daily basis during the summer months only. Despite record patronage, the three-day-a-week regime was reinstated for the winter. In the summer of 2007–2008 it was scheduled to operate daily. Sometimes Kiwis still get it wrong.

⑬ THE GRAFFITI EXPRESS: THE TRAIN TO WAITAKERE

AUCKLAND TO WAITAKERE

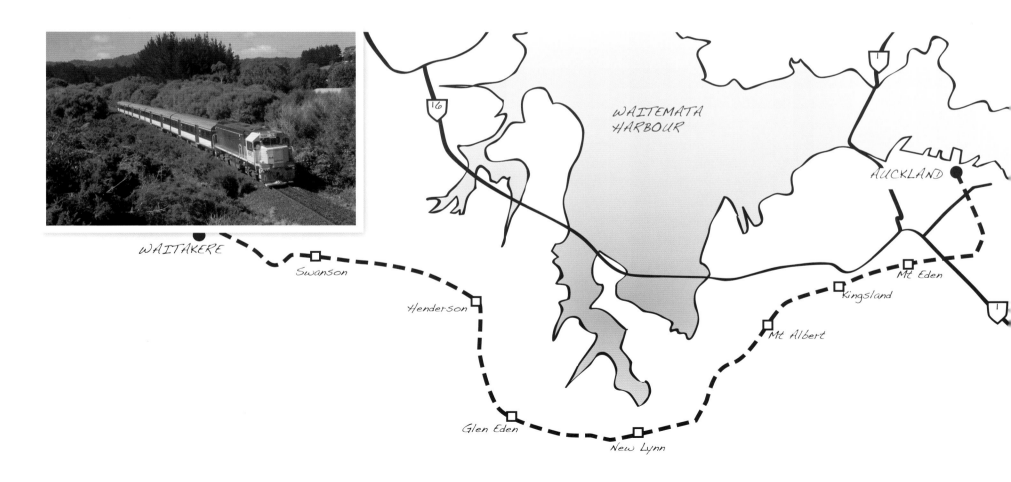

Auckland is not entirely bereft of suburban rail services. Despite the city's love affair with the motor car there have always been interesting passenger rail options. As the love affair sours because of Los Angeles-like traffic gridlock, Aucklanders are turning to the trains as an increasingly efficient means of commuter travel. And tourists are twigging to their advantages in terms of ease of transit, comfort and historical significance.

The Onehunga branch line no longer accommodates passenger trains, suburban or otherwise, yet it has more history than most. Pre-Main Trunk days, 1873 to be precise, saw its opening and it became a vital step in the contemporary journey from Auckland to Wellington. A boat train carried passengers out to the steamer waiting at Onehunga wharf, preparatory to an often turbulent passage down the coast to New Plymouth, and a connection with the New Plymouth-Wellington express that ran over tracks installed as long ago as 1886.

The southern line via Newmarket and Remuera eventually served as the principal suburban railway as far as Papakura. Later the eastern diversion, branching off at Westfield, and built in the more rail-friendly late 1920s, enabled trains to enter the city via its stunning maritime front door, the Waitemata Harbour waterfront.

The development of the Britomart site, the continued double-tracking of the western line and the recent unexpected rush of patronage to Auckland's suburban train services, make the return of suburban passenger trains to Onehunga along the oldest route of all, increasingly likely.

As historic as the southern route beyond Newmarket remains, and as picturesque as the eastern diversion along the waterfront approaches continues to be, it was the western line that took my fancy.

The new Auckland Britomart station is an atmospheric place to seek out a train to the west. I am waiting for the suburban service to take me to Waitakere. It's years since I've done this journey and because of the changes both at Britomart and, apparently, along the track, the trip promises much. Okay, so not a lot of new tracks are being built in New Zealand — yet — but the upgrading of existing lines like the Auckland to Waitakere is the next best thing.

Auckland Station has been through several incarnations. It was originally located in Queen Street near the Chief

Post Office. In fact it was twice located in this vicinity. In 1930 its centre of operation moved to Beach Road, at least ten minutes' walk from the CBD. It was a strange move, one that proved the doomsayers correct: fewer suburban passengers utilised rail options, at a time when motor cars were becoming more common.

After nearly 73 years trains returned to the heart of Auckland city. The Beach Road precinct is now called Strand Station. The old brick building is still standing but is now a student hostel.

'So you're off on the Graffiti Express,' said the young man wearing a green beanie and an enigmatic smirk. He'd been standing behind me at the ticket counter as I sought to buy my return ticket from a young woman kind enough to suggest I purchase an all-day suburban pass. An 'Adult Day Rover', no less. Perhaps she sensed that I was the sort who would be keen to cover the entire network. Obviously, at 11.00 am, I wasn't busting my gut to be anywhere in a hurry.

The train to Waitakere pulls impatiently away from the artificial glow of Britomart Transport Centre and up the rising stretch of tunnel track to the natural light. Inner-city apartments glower down as the line heads towards the old Beach Road railway station. Off to the left the sparkling waters of the Waitemata Harbour glint. A new curvature of track cuts sharply inland away from the harbour, bisecting the old Auckland Railway Station platforms, before linking up with the route that carries the train towards Newmarket. This new centre of diversion is known as Quay Park Junction. It is a work in progress.

The diversion to the western line serving Waitakere involves merging at Newmarket with the route that began life as the North Auckland railway. Freight trains still plod amiably towards New Zealand's subtropical north, centred on Whangarei, or curve down the branch line from Waiotira Junction south of Whangarei to the west coast town of Dargaville.

Beyond the tangle of rail developments immediately south-west of Britomart, it's comforting to make it through the old Parnell tunnel. Off to the left the headquarters of a steam-train excursion operator, Mainline Steam, reveals the snout of a restored steam engine — the sleek JA 1275 — peeking out of a maintenance shed. To the right the Auckland Domain, setting for the grand chambers of Auckland Museum, reaches down to the tree-lined border with the western rail corridor, as the train to Waitakere, a push-pull configuration, climbs towards Newmarket.

The Auckland Museum contains one of the world's best collections of Maori and Pacific art and Newmarket is an increasingly lively shopping precinct, reinvigorated like Parnell Village near the beginning of the line. Further on the Auckland Zoo and an ambitious transport and technology museum, known as MOTAT, can be accessed along the route of the Waitakere train.

A signal box just this side of Newmarket has a splash of semi-circular graffiti that looks like subtropical fungal growth adorning its woodwork.

The green beanie guy is right about the graffiti. The western line to Waitakere provides more exposure for the tagging artists of Auckland than any other line I've seen. Fellow passengers sigh at the sight of railside business premises daubed with spraypainted slogans, logos and

Graffiti artists have left their controversial mark near Mount Eden Station.

OPPOSITE Kingsland on the western line: the new face of Auckland suburban stations.

mother with a Scottish accent and three young daughters refers to the guard laughingly as Thomas the Tank Engine as he collects her ticket. The two schoolgirls rabbit on about manipulating their mothers' time-lines and curfews to facilitate the simple act of wagging school.

Newmarket Station. This is the junction for lines that head south and west. The south line was once part of the North Island Main Trunk before the deviation from Westfield via Glen Innes and the Auckland waterfront came into being.

The western line, which doubles as the Northland route, heads back out through an urban tunnel that burrows beneath huge car park buildings as the city closes in. In a reversal of traditional mating calls, young women in their lunch hour can be seen whistling and waving at construction workers in their hard hats before the train passes Mount Eden Prison, where a guard mans a watchtower overlooking the line, and Eden Park, scene of All Black rugby glory, before pulling into Kingsland station.

If you happen to be English — or Scottish — the revamped Kingsland Station may bring on a bout of homesickness. In recent times it has been completely rebuilt and realigned, with double tracks and fixtures straight out of station models found on the Newcastle to Carlisle branch through Northumberland. Rugby test-match specials used to discharge their cargo of inebriated fans at Kingsland in days when trains were charged with the sacred duty of transporting downcountry All Black adherents to the test-match citadel of Eden Park. In 2007 Kingsland Station represents the new face of suburban station architecture. Eden Park still looms on the suburban

the figments of idle minds. Concrete block retaining walls, wooden poster boards, loop-line buffers, railway maintenance sheds — any unmonitored surface has been subjected to the colourful ramblings of the urban underground free-range artist. Some of the graffiti is ornate, although far be it from me to encourage these nocturnal scoundrels to deface other peoples' property. But you have to admire the taggers' efficiency. Even a lump of concrete no bigger than a football has been tagged.

The quietly-spoken guard is locked into a discussion with two schoolgirls who justify their presence on the train by saying they've missed the school bus. A young

A half-naked man tends his garden, oblivious to the train. An older woman passenger with a Helen Shapiro bouffant gets the giggles.

skyline, but somehow it has lost its omnipotence.

The line heads south-west as the graffiti intensifies. Mount Albert passes and soon suburban Avondale is upon us. Located on an uplifted ridge, Avondale Station, as mothers fold pushchairs and youths push dark glasses to their spike-haired heads, reveals sweeping views of the western suburbs and, off in the heat-hazy distance, the foothills of the Waitakeres.

'I told you there was a lot of graffiti,' the green beanie, having changed seats in the now-crowded carriage, reiterates.

The train heads due south for a time, before arcing around through New Lynn and on to Glen Eden, with its beautifully restored, salmon-pink, old-world station and wooded enclosures. 'Meat City', a large butchery in New Lynn, recalls the John Lennon song of the same name. New Lynn calls up too the chain of Auckland suburban names apparently linked by a common theme — New Lynn, Grey Lynn, Glen Eden, Glen Innes . . . A mural of a steam engine at New Lynn, affirming our mode of transport and right of passage, although the taggers have gone perilously close to smudging the image of what looks like a classic old AB

Pacific, is reassuring. Perhaps Auckland taggers have a code of ethics and recognise certain boundaries.

The double-tracking of the line between New Lynn and Henderson was opened recently with all due ceremony. Helen Clark, the Prime Minister, who was very much part of the 1980s Labour Government that accelerated the demise of rail services (perhaps she was away that day), attended the opening of the new extension. There are now plans to electrify the route as not only the constricting Auckland road traffic gridlock, but environmental imperatives, force the hand of officialdom.

We are in 'Westie' country now, a pocket of the greater Auckland area that has more than its fair share of freedom-loving, independent-minded inhabitants. Perhaps it's the rugged, forested hills and wild ocean beaches that have made Westies the way they are. Certainly there are enough writers, artists, visionaries and characters out west to complement the area's appeal.

As if on cue, at Fruitvale Road Station a middle-aged man wearing half-mast jeans and Andy Capp hat and shoulder bag climbs aboard. At Swanson, where again the station is beautifully restored, a young blonde-haired woman with a self-deprecating air swings aboard and finds a seat opposite me. 'Bloody hell, I nearly broke a nail,' she declares, while the guard, a more jovial version than the Auckland central to Newmarket clone, clicks her ticket.

A lone pukeko wanders along the ballast beyond Swanson. A half-naked man tends his garden, oblivious to the train. An older woman passenger with a Helen Shapiro bouffant gets the giggles. The train has been

OPPOSITE 'Westies' wait at Glen Eden to board the 'Graffiti Express'.

arcing due north beyond Sunnydale and is now heading out west again. Perhaps that's why fellow passengers seem more relaxed; they're Westies. You half expect Ewen Gilmour and other popular entertainers from this neck of the woods, to clamber aboard in genre-defying outfits. Henderson, Sturges Road and Ranui Stations have already been and gone, with increasing numbers of Westies climbing aboard and heading further west.

Groups of Aucklanders and visiting tourists take the train these days to visit the Henderson Valley and Kumeu wineries. West Auckland was the birthplace of New Zealand's growing reputation as a leading wine producer. Although Marlborough, Gisborne and Hawke's Bay now have the edge, the Henderson Valley was the original home of New Zealand wine-making.

From the Waitakere tunnel it is possible to look back and see the Skytower in downtown Auckland. The train to Waitakere may have taken us out of our comfort zone but it's typical of travel in New Zealand that, just when you think you have made it to another physical dimension, you are reminded how close to home you are.

One of the most appealing features of the train to Waitakere is its destination. Getting there is half the fun of course, but to end up in a region where over-lapping road access routes lead to the forests and walkways of the Waitakere Ranges, and the fingerling arteries beyond to the West Coast beaches of Whatipu, Karekare, Piha, White's Beach, Bethells Beach and Muriwai, adds an extra something to the rail link.

Route 24, the Waitakere Scenic Drive, begins at Titirangi, an attractive outer suburb set in the foothills, and extends north towards Swanson and the line's railhead at Waitakere. Travellers leave the train at either of these stations in a wooded hinterland far removed from the built-up inner city and suburban clusters.

Auckland, well known for its twin harbours of Waitemata and Manukau with their gently lapping coves and bays, has a wilder maritime side. The Waitakere train and the connecting Scenic Drive and no-exit west coast roads lead to crashing surf on rugged beaches backed by unspoiled bush and forests that could be a thousand miles from the gentle beaches fringing the built-up areas to the east.

Waitakere is an odd location to conclude a riveting train ride. There's not much here. A few houses, a decidedly humble station, a continuation of the line carrying on around the bend to the north. When the train to Waitakere comes to a stop, almost in the middle of nowhere, at least there's another train to keep us company. A log freighter from the north has been waiting for our train to arrive. Its presence seems to arouse logistical concern. It could delay our departure on the return journey, according to a worried looking Westie.

'How long before this train heads back to the city?' I ask the train manager while stretching my legs along the modest platform.

'Just as long as it takes the driver to change ends.'

It doesn't take more than five minutes and soon the train from Waitakere is ghosting back to the east, through the Waitakere tunnel and on the downhill slide all the way back to Britomart.

It would have been wonderful to be able to wait

at Waitakere Station for a passenger service heading north, but such trains no longer run on a regular basis. To travel beyond Auckland into the subtropical reaches of Northland by train was a rare privilege. I was lucky enough to enjoy such services once, on railcars and mixed goods trains in the years before the hammer of passenger service curtailment came down.

In 2007 it's all a matter of excursion trains. Because freight connections continue to ply the far-north lines, the right of passage is still sometimes available. Excursion operations exercise Northland rail options and although they are not as frequent as rail fans would like, they roll around often enough.

There has even been talk of extending the train to Waitakere as far as Helensville, a Kaipara Harbour-based township that already houses Auckland commuters who drive as far as the Waitakere railhead to catch existing trains to Auckland.

Beyond Helensville the Northland line hugs the shoreline of the Kaipara Harbour, through Kaukapakapa, then heads inland to Wellsford before continuing north around the outer reaches of the harbour, through Maungaturoto, across country to Waiotira Junction and the branch to Dargaville on the northern Wairoa River, followed by a north-eastern main line shift to the east coast and Northland's leading centre, Whangarei.

Many excursions pinpoint Whangarei as their destination, but others carry on north to Otiria, location of another branch junction that used to see railcars heading west, through Kaikohe to the railhead at Okaihau.

A vintage rail endeavour, the Bay of Islands Vintage Railway, used to operate trains from Kawakawa to Opua, but while it is not functional at present, there are promising signs of resurrection.

The Opua Express was taken for granted in the 1950s, a means of transporting tourists to the mystical Bay of Islands after they'd travelled through the mangrove swamps and around the tidal estuaries of the Northland rail network. Not long after goods services finally ceased on the Opua branch, a rail enthusiasts' excursion ran from Auckland, via Waitakere, to the Bay of Islands. The train went all the way. The two DA diesel engines empowered with hauling the excursion rumbled out on to the Opua wharf to touch base with the dead end of a line that has become part of New Zealand rail folklore.

As a footnote to the ride, out and back, on the train to Waitakere, and the reaffirmation of existing suburban services at last in Auckland, expressions of intent have been lodged regarding a totally new line to bring New Zealand's leading city into line with international equivalents. An extension of the soon-to-be-resurrected Onehunga branch is mooted. Beyond Onehunga the new line would link Auckland Airport with the city's suburban network, via Onehunga and Penrose, thereby easing passenger access to and from the airport.

Meanwhile the ongoing double-tracking of the line to Waitakere, and the commitment to eventual electrification, are signs of the times — finally, a concession to the advantages of rail travel.

BIBLIOGRAPHY

Bromby, Robin, *Rails that Built a Nation*. Grantham House, Wellington, 2003.

Churchman, Geoffrey B., *On the TranzAlpine Trail*. Transpress NZ, Wellington, 2004.

Churchman, Geoffrey B. & Hurst, Tony, *The Railways of New Zealand*. Transpress NZ, Wellington, 1990.

Frame, Janet, *An Angel at my Table*. Hutchinson, Auckland, 1984.

Garner, John, *Guide to New Zealand Rail Heritage*. IPL Books, Wellington, 1996.

Hurst, Tony, *The Kingston Flyer Line: A History*. Transpress NZ, Wellington, 2004.

Leitch, D.B., *Engine Pass — New Zealand Railways*. AH & AW Reed, Wellington, 1967.

Mellor, Peter J., *New Zealand Railway Reflections*. NZ Railway and Locomotive Society Inc., Wellington, 1995.

Meyer, R.J., *All Aboard — The Ships and Trains that Served Lake Wakatipu*. NZ Railway and Locomotive Society Inc., Wellington, 1980.

Miller, F. W. G., *The Story of the Kingston Flyer*. Whitcoulls Ltd, Auckland, 1975.

New Zealand Railfan Magazine (various editions), Triple M Publications, Wellington.

Pierre, Bill, *North Island Main Trunk*. AH & AW Reed, Wellington, 1981.

Rous-Marten, Charles, *New Zealand Railways to 1900*. NZ Railway and Locomotive Society Inc., Wellington, 1985.

Stewart, W.W., *Grand Old Days of Steam*. AH & AW Reed, Wellington, 1975.

Troup, Gordon, *Footplate, The Victorian Engineman's New Zealand*. AH & AW Reed, Wellington, 1975.

Walter, David, *Stratford — Shakespearian Town under the Mountain, A History*. Dunmore Publishing, Wellington, 2005.